CHRONICLES OF

# *Barrington*

# ILLINOIS

DIANE P. KOSTICK

*Foreword by Karen Darch, Illustrations by Mort Luby*

THE
History
PRESS

Published by The History Press
Charleston, SC
www.historypress.net

*Front cover*: White House. *Painting by Mort Luby.*
*Back cover, top left*: Catlow Theater today. *Painting by Mort Luby*; *top right*: Armed Forces Monument at Evergreen Cemetery. *Photo by the author*; *bottom*: Fire wagons at a Fourth of July Parade. *Courtesy of Barrington Fire Department.*

Unless otherwise noted, photos are by the author.

First published 2015

Manufactured in the United States

ISBN 978.1.46711.917.7

Library of Congress Control Number: 2015952224

*Notice*: The information in this book is true and complete to the best of our knowledge. It is offered without guarantee on the part of the author or The History Press. The author and The History Press disclaim all liability in connection with the use of this book.

*To Andy, who is never far away. To Alden, Bode and Xander, who waited in the car while I took pictures to "fill-in-the-blanks," who waited for lunch while I edited one more page and who shared in my mission.*

# Contents

# *Foreword*

How fitting that Diane Kostick should publish her *Chronicles of Barrington, Illinois* during this sesquicentennial year for our village. Through the pages that follow, the village and many of its colorful inhabitants over the years come alive and give us a glimpse of the simplicity and greatness that has made Barrington a wonderful community for a century and a half. Through biographies of sports figures, artists, writers, military veterans, conservationists, political activists, playwrights, opera stars, recyclers and just everyday "do-gooders," we come to understand how Barrington came to be not just another town on the prairie but a place beloved by those who have had the good fortune to reside here—whether for a few years or a lifetime. These are "Barrington folk" who in return gave much to their hometown and their neighbors.

*Chronicles of Barrington* does more than spotlight the characters who have called Barrington home. This work also reminds us of the many institutions and businesses that have helped to weave the fabric of the community. The Jewel Tea Company, Good Shepherd Hospital, Lipofsky's Store, Pepper Construction Company, the Barrington Library—with its many growth spurts—and many churches and schools are all so much a part of what makes Barrington, Barrington. Understanding how and why these institutions came to be is an education not to be missed.

As you read this work, I hope it will give you a new appreciation for the faces and places of our corner of the Chicago region. It is with utmost gratitude for her enthusiasm, time, effort and attention to detail that, on behalf of Barrington, I thank Diane Kostick for this valuable, thoughtful and endearing chronicle of a community that is so special to so many, particularly as we celebrate Barrington's 150th birthday.

Karen Darch
Village President of Barrington
July 1, 2015

# *Acknowledgements*

No one who writes a book can write it alone. It takes the kindness and assistance of others—family, friends and/or colleagues—to write a book. This has truly been the case in putting together the *Chronicles of Barrington, Illinois*. My thanks to each individual and/or family who responded to my phone calls, e-mails or in-person requests for you to edit the written materials related to you for accuracy and an appropriate tone. Your changes and comments were invaluable. Thanks, too, for the images and documents you provided, for your poems, stories and personal histories. Thanks to my manuscript editors and to those who assisted with scanning photos and formatting the text. You all were my guardian angels who made this book happen.

Listed below are some of the people who contributed with research, editing and encouragement to bring *Chronicles of Barrington* into existence. My thanks to each of you.

Thomas Balsamo
Barrington Area Library: Rose, Kate, Eileen, Gwen and other Adult Services
	staff
Barrington Township
Peter and Michael Bateman
George Bessett
Sheryl Campen
Community Church of Barrington

# ACKNOWLEDGEMENTS

Paul Corwin
Cuba Township
Karen Darch
Dan Delcore
Bruce Dockery
Ela Township Historical Society and Museum
Dave Engle
John and Jim Feit
Ken Gebbhart
Jenni Hart
Karl Heitman
Sally Houlihan
Mike and Joyce Karon
Susan Anderson Khleif
Curt Larson
Ginny Newman
Susan (Young) Parks
Joe Sanchez
Andy Schaefer
Sandy Schroeder
Janet Souter
Steven Stamatis
Tina Stoval
Tamara Tabel
Don Thompson Jr.
Sandy Vanderburg
Jennifer Yuen

# *Introduction*

*Our identity as a community is shaped by our stories.*
*—Anonymous*

D rive through the Barrington area and you'll see a land dotted with hills, valleys, streams, rivers, lakes and wetlands, dressed with flora and fauna typical of the Midwest. However, geography alone doesn't begin to represent the diversity of Barrington's history, people and development. Its fifty-five-thousand-plus inhabitants come from wildly different backgrounds and social classes. Some descended from European immigrants, residents of New England who ventured west in search of a better life—ready to work hard, develop new roots and establish their new farms, businesses and a village. Others, more recent arrivals, saw the Barrington area's promise as a vibrant community and used their unique talents to keep it moving forward into the twenty-first century. Still others reached their potential after benefiting from Barrington's fine schools and went on to greatness in sports, commerce and the arts.

Individuals profiled in the chapters of this book represent people who have worked hard to place themselves in a plethora of professions, trades and careers. Some have gained national renown; some are admired locally. All are pioneers in one sense or another, and all have called Barrington home for all or part of their lives. In many ways, Barrington is a typical suburb built on Illinois prairie land, but its history is a treasure-trove of untold tales, hidden personal memories and area lore. This book presents

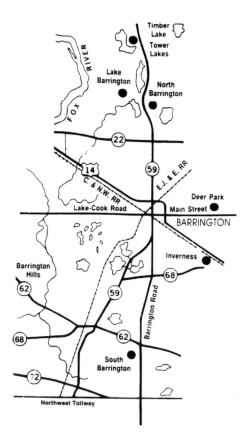

Map of Barrington. *Courtesy of Barrington Chamber of Commerce.*

a portrait of those whose vision, resourcefulness and dedication contributed to the strength and character of the Barrington Area—its families, companies, horse farms and downtown. It is a compliment to their heritage, education, concern for natural spaces, use of recreational areas, charity and faith that unites these diverse villages and people.

A book of this nature is required to include some and exclude others due to space limitations. In researching sources for this book, I have met amazing people who have done remarkable deeds—helped orchestrate the 1933 World's Fair, contributed to Chicago's gangster mythology and taken center stage in our nation's sports' glory, art venues and mass media communication. Join me in following these fascinating citizens who make Barrington the enclave that it is today—an energetic place to live, work and play. They are people who know the importance of hard work that is needed to succeed. These are stories that need to be told so they won't be forgotten.

I

# *History*

*The history of the world is but the biography of great men.*
*—Thomas Carly*

In 1830, at the urging of President Andrew Jackson, Congress enacted his Indian Removal Act, giving him the authority to negotiate treaties with Indians in order to force them to relocate. Jackson's tenacity in following this policy brought about a dramatic remapping of the nascent western lands.

In T. Andreas's 1884 *History of Cook County, Illinois—Earliest Period to the Present*, the chapter on Barrington indicates:

> *Prior to 1834 very few, if any, white men visited Barrington. In that year, Jesse F. Miller and William Van Orsdal arrived. Much to their surprise there were 500 Potawatomi still living in the groves along the banks of the Spring Creek—an area recognized for its abundant wild game and fish, fruits and vegetables. In 1835, these men were joined by Benjamin Irick, Henry Clawson and Philip Hawley. Little is known beyond the names of these hearty souls.*

Each year thereafter more settlers came and started homesteading.

Records show that, after the Blackhawk War of 1832, an agreement was signed by representatives of the Potawatomi, Chippewa and Ottawa tribes with the federal government. On September 26, 1833, at a powwow held on Ela Flat in Deer Grove, Native Americans *agreed* to move west of

These Native American arrowheads found in the Barrington area are estimated to be 800 to 1,500 years old. Potawatomi, Ottawas and Chippewas lived in the area.

the Mississippi River. Government agents supplied the Indians with plenty of whiskey, *persuading* the Indians to relinquish their lands to Washington by August 1836 in return for an annual grant of $100,000.

On the heels of the treaty, the threat of Indian attacks subsided and people were encouraged to move westward. By the mid-1830s, white settlers began to arrive in Barrington Township. Miller and Van Orsdal chose the location to take advantage of the vast amount of timber in the area that they would saw down to build their houses, barns, sheds, corncribs and even fences. In addition, they would clear part of the tree groves to develop their farms, which are now located in Barrington Hills.

Upon their arrival, however, they were startled to see five hundred Potawatomi still residing in Miller Grove, land that would ultimately become Barrington Center. Ironically, fearful of the pioneers, the Indians fled, making way for more easterners to immigrate. These earliest pioneers included Benjamin Irick, Henry Clawson, A.C. Bucklin, E.N. Miller, Benjamin Richardson, Gilbert A. Applebee, William H. Otis, Homer Wilmarth, L.O.E. Manning, George S. Browning, Henry Smith, Alvah Miller and Philip Hawley. Some of the men came alone; others brought their families. They arrived overland in canvas-covered wagons or by longboats traveling along the Great Lakes river system and then overland. Their journeys were difficult and dangerous and took several months. But the lure of rich prairie soil, abundant water and reasonable land prices brought these industrious families to the area. Most of these men became the backbone of the community, serving in numerous capacities, including on school, government, social, church and planning boards. Their efforts set the tone and direction for the community. Some of these original settlers have descendants living in the community today, and many of them still have tales of Old Barrington to tell.

These early immigrants came with modest possessions: food, clothing and scant pieces of furniture. They also brought tools, bedding, kitchen utensils, kettles, rifles, tent supplies and farming equipment, including plows, hoes and bailing instruments. The pioneers had high hopes of a better life. The trip west was fraught with dangers of death, wagon wrecks and Indian attacks. Only the bravest succeeded and only by the grace of God. The time chosen to begin their journey was critical. If they left too early, they might not find enough spring grasses for their livestock; if they left too late, they could be dogged by winter snowstorms.

*Right*: The Applebee House was constructed in 1855 and burned to the ground in 1888. It was rebuilt on top of the original foundation. Three families lived in the house: Applebee, Wiseman and Holtzee.

*Below*: An undated postcard view of the Kraus Grocery Store, which served customers in Cuba, now Cuba Township. *Postcard courtesy of Ken Gebhardt.*

Many pioneers of the area were eastern Yankees followed by the English, German or Irish settlers. They were of a sturdy stock who came to put down roots and grow families. They cleared the prairie, planted crops, raised livestock and settled in, determined to carve out a prosperous future for themselves and their offspring.

The first frame house was constructed in 1841 by S.W. Kingsley, but by the mid-1840s, numerous log cabins dotted the countryside, built by John Catlow, Philip Hawley, Ebin Conant and others. The 1840 federal census showed that sixty-one families were living in the Barrington Precinct, as it was then called.

These Yankees planned to establish a new community that would unite the farmers. They built the first schoolhouse and formed Barrington Center, founding a village. At the direction of the county sheriff, the inhabitants assembled at the home of William Otis and selected the name Barrington for their township; the name chosen was probably influenced by the large number of people who originated from Greater Barrington, Massachusetts.

The Illinois and Wisconsin Railroad was extended to Deer Grove by 1852, and in 1854, the village hired Robert C. Campbell as its chief engineer. He was tasked with creating a city plan that would consider the impact of the extension of the railroad. His design allowed for the building of homes in an orderly manner once the rail lines became operational. The community continued to expand with the Illinois and Wisconsin Railroad situated at the intersection of Ela Road and Northwest Highway. Needing more property, the railroad acquired forty acres of land from Benjamin Felter in 1854 and began laying the new rail.

Engineer Campbell was commissioned to plot out a *proper* plan for the creation of the village. Familiar with the English measurement system of chains and links, he platted the village into blocks and lots within an eight-acre radius. The first plots sold were in the city center and became Barrington's core. By the 1870s, the village promoted sales of lots ranging from $1 to $500. Ads promoted that the lots were "located on clean streets line with hardy maples." In 1889, with the establishment of the Elgin, Joliet & Eastern Railroad (EJ&E) just west of the town center, the village continued to grow. Weary of city congestion, crime and decay, urban residents flocked to the open spaces and the fresh air of the bucolic countryside. Barrington burgeoned. Businesses sprang up near the railroads to serve local companies and to supply goods to the increasing number of farm families and townspeople flooding into the area.

A typical midwestern farmstead. The rich soil provided families with food and a place for friends to gather for picnics, barn dances and quilting bees.

Railroad Street in Barrington appears quite muddy in this postcard. It cost one cent to mail the card. *Postcard courtesy of Tina Stoval.*

After an election was held on November 18, 1863, documents necessary to establish a municipality were written for Barrington's incorporation. The Illinois legislature granted the Town of Barrington a charter on February 16, 1865, but the Civil War delayed the charter's completion. On March 20, the new village elected its first five trustees: Homer Wilmarth, M.B. McIntosh,

A.K. Van Gorder, Oscar Lawrence and Gottleib Heimerdinder. Standing committees of trustees and clerks were set in place by a vote of 57 "yes" and 0 "no," and by April 10, rules of order and regulations for governing the town were also adopted. Barrington's first mayor, Homer Wilmarth, was appointed for a one-year term, and in 1866, Millius B. McIntosh was elected mayor by a vote of Barrington's citizens. Barrington Station, as the village was first called, officially became the Village of Barrington.

Tom Creet established a blacksmith shop at the southeast corner of Baldwin and Schaumburg Roads. Later, Creet realized the advantage of being in the city center; his shop, the family home and their household possessions were moved on a flatbed rail car into the village, relocating to the corner of Cook and Station Streets. On their way to and from school, children often stood outside the building watching the blacksmiths in leather aprons hammer red-hot metal on enormous black anvils as they forged metal tools, farm implements and horseshoes, as well as latches and hinges of every sort. Blacksmiths kept the wheels of the community rolling. When farm tools broke down, obtaining repair parts might take days or weeks while grains stood in fields waiting to be harvested. Local blacksmiths, like Creet and Wichman, stepped in and could pull an obsolete repair part out of a junk pile and make it over to fit the needed repair. These artisans were in great demand and highly respected.

On long winter evenings, homeowners with a modicum of woodworking and carpentry skills fashioned door handles, drawer pulls, bowls, spoons, forks and other household necessities for their families' needs. Farming wasn't easy, but it was a good life.

By the end of the nineteenth century, Barrington boasted many shops and services. It became a trading and transportation center for people living in communities in the surrounding countryside. Shops included Louis Schroeder's Hardware Store, Bela Abbott's Carpentry Shop, Hank Abbot's Drug Store and Watch Repair and Parker's Drug and Jewelry Shop. The community soon added M.B. McIntosh's Lumber Company, Leroy Powers' General Merchandise Store, Chas Jahnke Livery Stable, Henning's Saloon and John C. Plagge's General Store. Plagge's shop also hosted a dentist's office upstairs for Dr. Charles Coltrin, in addition to an office for the justice of the peace, Homer Wilmarth, and an undertaker's parlor.

In addition, the post office, which had been located in a home on the outskirts of town, was repositioned near the train station. On June 14, 1904, mail delivery began from the post office that is now on South Cook Street. Horse and buggy carriers included Charles Hutchinson, Samuel Landwer,

Five generations of Wichmans have lived in Barrington. These blacksmith tools have been part of the family's collection for years.

Ben Freye and Herman Gieske. The horse-drawn mail routes were between twenty-five and twenty-eight miles long; with the advent of the automobile, routes increased to forty miles. These added amenities ensured a steady flow of new arrivals to the Barrington area.

People from nearby villages moved into Barrington to be near the railroad station and close to stores that served their needs. Like most towns of the day, in wet weather, the village center morphed into a sea of muck and mud. Wooden crosswalks provided residents with some protection from the elements, but mud often rose between the plank sidewalks, rendering the walkways slippery and treacherous.

Horses provided transportation to and from town. Hitching posts lined the streets and were visible in front of most homes. Four town pumps and four troughs provided water for the waiting animals. Sometimes a runaway horse and buggy broke the quiet of the village as the team raced through the streets. Men flailing their arms attempted to quell the pair, but more often than not, the horse and buggy were upended and the contents of the wagon spilled onto the dirt road.

Businesses introduced two social necessities: benches and awnings. Benches allowed customers to sit and share news with neighbors and friends. Sturdy sailcloth awnings enabled shopkeepers to set their wares outdoors and also protected shoppers from inclement weather.

Twin Sister's Painted-Lady home on Lake Street. *Painting by Mort Luby*.

Earlier houses were cottage-type or small one-and-a-half-story structures. Cackling hens and crowing roosters filled the morning air. Most families also kept a cow and a pig. Sometimes petitions were circulated asking the village board to banish a pig and its pen from the neighborhood as that odor quickly escalated to a stench on stifling hot summer days. Picket fences surrounded homes to keep animals confined. When animals did stray, they were housed in the village pound. Owners could reclaim their livestock or pets after they paid the pound master a set fee.

Settlers illuminated their homes with tallow candles and kerosene lamps and warmed the interiors with open fireplaces. Cooking was done in the fireplace or on a wood-burning stove. Iron kettles hung from movable rods that swung over the fire. Baked goods were prepared in a hole in the wall built into the fireplace.

Unfortunately, fires were common occurrences that struck most residents with terror. Firefighting equipment did not exist in the village. Water was available only from a nearby stream or well. Fires had to burn themselves out unless a bucket brigade could be formed in time to extinguish the flames. Many fires resulted in a total loss of the building and all of the property inside. In the business section, fires were disastrous as flames spread from one wooden structure to the next.

In 1890, a major fire erupted downtown, killing one and destroying an entire block of buildings. Just eight years later, a blaze swept east to the railroad tracks, consuming a second block of businesses. Aghast by the rash of fires, townspeople took action. They formed a fire department on June 15, 1898, and thirty-seven volunteers joined. Citizens also voted to dig a city well and erect a standpipe on top of the hill at the corner of Hillside and Hough Streets. Water mains, hydrants and a reservoir well were installed behind city hall. Barrington's first piece of fire equipment was purchased. The rig carried fifty yards of hoses and two brass nozzles. Edward J. Heise was the first firefighter of the community, and John Frommelkamp was the first fire marshal. At the clang of the Zion Church bell, men sprang into action for weekly fire drills held on Main Street. If a fire broke out, shrill whistles mounted on top of the Bowman Dairy and Gieske's Steam Laundry sounded the alarm.

In the same year, the telephone company installed poles and lines for twenty subscribers. By 1904, telephone customers could make long-distance calls to Palatine and Fox River Grove. Later, Barrington resident Mary Ann Bue Thompson served as an operator in the facility for many years before retiring. A power plant was built at the end of Harrison Street to generate

Barrington Fire Department poses for a group photo in May 1963 to celebrate its 100th birthday. *Photo courtesy of Barrington Fire Department.*

Tony Thompson (left) and Jeff Larsen (right) represent today's firefighters, who are also trained paramedics and serve an expansive Barrington community.

electricity to provide the town with public lighting. Strings of lights were draped across the streets at each intersection. The incandescent lights were extinguished at 11:00 p.m. and not turned back on until dawn.

As Barrington's population increased, so did the number of businesses and industries. The American Malleable Iron Works was constructed in 1898 but went bankrupt two years later due to inferior casting. A village hall was built in 1899, and by the 1900s, residents were enjoying motion pictures shown on the second floor. The Barrington Steam Laundry opened in 1900 and experienced immediate success. Around this time, the First State Bank of Barrington was also established. It stood at the corner of Cook Street and Park Avenue and remained in place for decades. After many unsuccessful rebirths, today, it is the home of McGonigal's Irish Pub.

The twentieth century saw a period of rapid development. In 1929, Barrington established the position of police chief and bought its first squad car. Ernest W. Baade served as chief from 1929 until 1950. The village also purchased its first two-way radio system in 1948. The police department was located on the second floor of the village hall until 1951, when the department required additional space to adequately serve its citizens.

First State Bank of Barrington. *Painting by Mort Luby.*

As the community flourished, so did the need to borrow books. William J. Cameron offered a section of his drugstore for that purpose. The library stayed there for several years until the collection exceeded the capacity. At the urging of the Barrington's Women's Club, the library was moved to a room on Cook Street over George Wagner's Market and later to the Village Hall on Hough Street. Members of the Women's Club served as librarians, and by 1926, a library board was elected. According to Arnett C. Lines's *History of Barrington*, "The library was funded by a grant from Mrs. Caroline (George) Ela and Frank Hecht who donated $1,000.00 in memory of his mother. Many books were donated from personal libraries." In 1953, a bond was issued to build a more permanent library at the corners of Hough and Monument Streets. The Williamsburg-style edifice became the new home when the library moved into its new, larger home, now the offices of the Barrington Township and food depository. By 1956, the library boasted of a collection of eleven thousand books. Citizens' needs for more library service resulted in approval of a bond issue in 1975 for a new and enlarged site. The library opened its doors to patrons in 1978. By 1993, the library provided sixty thousand square feet of space for its ever-growing collection. In 2013 and 2014, the Barrington Area Library underwent a major renovation—no space was added, but the building witnessed its spaces rearranged to better serve its patrons and house its materials.

Barrington celebrated its centennial in 1963 with a year-long schedule of activities. Many events took place during the week of July 3–10, including historical walking tours, lectures and displays around town. The city also sponsored parades, hot dog picnics and a beard-growing contest. Many townsmen soon resembled the heavily bearded men of Lincoln's times. Local firemen joined in on the fun and challenged one another to grow the longest beard.

On October 25, 1960, less than two weeks before the presidential election, John F. Kennedy stood on the front steps of Barrington High School (BHS) to seek the support of local Democrats. Kennedy came at the invitation of his friend George Ross Kennedy (no relation to the senator), a former PT109 crewman, to pitch his run for the presidency. A large crowd greeted Kennedy's entourage. Bright banners supporting Kennedy were mixed with a handful of signs supporting Richard Nixon, the Republican presidential candidate. Kennedy's scheduled appearance in the area, a largely Republican enclave, became the talk of the town for weeks leading up to the senator's election to the Oval Office.

Barrington Area Library. The first library was located in 1915 above William Cameron's drugstore.

Recently, original photos of Kennedy's visit were donated to BHS by 1962 alumna Joyce Tallion, who discovered them while reviewing family albums. Her then thirteen-year-old freshman brother, Rusty Anderson, a strong Kennedy fan, could have taken the black-and-white pictures of the young senator. At the November 21, 2013 Kennedy Photo Presentation Ceremony, Tallion said, "I thought this was the perfect place for these pictures." Retired Prairie Middle School principal Don Thompson noted that Kennedy "had great appeal to the youth at this time."

Current BHS principal, Steve McWilliams, said, "The photos are a great addition to the high school." Former superintendent Tom Leonard said, "For Barrington, [these pictures] coming here [on the day before the fiftieth anniversary of Kennedy's assassination] is a big moment."

Ray Wichman, a fifth-generation Barringtonian, told Tarah Thorne, a reporter for *Barrington Suburban Life*, "I remember a rather large crowd, but it was a lot of students and Barrington was primarily a Republican town." Wichman does remember Kennedy's visit as the senator spoke to the gathered audience. Few photos were taken that day because kids did not have cameras, let alone cellphones, commented Wichman. This makes Tallion's's collection all the more valuable. Joan Quinn is quoted as saying she "was overtly political, but he [Kennedy] was good looking…and I thought he was going to win."

In 1968, the Barrington Historical Society (now Museum) was formed to collect and house local memorabilia, including items saved when the first village school, Hough Street, fell to a wrecking ball to make way for a new building. The Historical Museum has been pivotal in preserving Barrington culture and village artifacts for generations. Its campus continues to grow and draws visitors from Barrington, other communities and nearby states.

The 1970s brought a decade of efforts to protect the countryside and preserve the lifestyle of Barringtonians. To that end, BACOG—the Barrington Area Council of Governments—was established as a planning tool for development and transportation, as well as the conservation of land and the protection of the environment. Donald Klein was named BACOG's first executive director. Of the organization, Klein said, "The coalition of local village governments has successfully preserved the quality of the environment, ecological balance and made the best use of local lands."

Joyce Tallion shares with the audience how she recently discovered original Senator Kennedy photos while browsing through old family photo albums. Her brother Rusty, a JFK fan, snapped the pictures.

In 1972, a site was proposed for a Barrington-area hospital at Route 22, west of Route 59; a permit was issued to the Evangelical Hospital Association. And in 1973, Quaker Oats donated ninety acres for the establishment of Good Shepherd Hospital (GSH). GSH's dedication took place on September 23, 1979. Today, it continues to expanded exponentially, offering citizens award-winning healthcare services.

Environmental issues dominated Barrington's concerns in the 1980s. Traffic congestion through the downtown area remained a sore spot among citizens and became fodder for politicians, who were eager to please constituents. As of 2015, the traffic issue has yet to be resolved by either the village or the state, and in the most recent village survey, it remains the number one complaint of Barrington residents.

Growing concern about diminished open land led nearby Cuba Township officials to create an "open space district" of more than seven hundred acres. Citizens still adhere to a philosophy of strict environmental guardianship as a prime focus of living in and around Barrington. There are numerous organizations that serve as watchful stewards of the serene landscape.

When Mark Beaubien retired as Cuba Township supervisor to serve as an Illinois senator in November 1996, David Nelson was appointed to the vacated position. Pricilla H. Rose became clerk at the same time. She and Dave Nelson continue in these roles to this day.

Taking note of the residents' demand for better sustainable living, the village started recycling plastics during the 1970s. In addition, the ever-expanding Park District agreed to seek bids on an eighteen-hole miniature golf course for Langendorf Park, increasing the popularity of the village recreation facilities. Four decades later, the residents responded to the need to expand the Park District offerings and voted to buy land that once served as the Jewel Tea Company Headquarters. The Park District turned the site into a vibrant venue for a variety of recreational activities like bike and walking trails, a "living treehouse," outdoor gathering spaces for clubs

A first-in-the-state treehouse at Citizens Park was made possible by a generous donation from the Pepper family. Residents can host children's parties or family reunions in the house.

and organizations, tennis facilities, a picnic area, a site for weddings and receptions, as well as other uses.

The 1970s saw the end of one of Barrington's most popular eateries. Charlotte's Pizza Parlor was closed by the state to widen Highway Route 14 and to correct an urgent safety issue. Locals lamented the demise of the restaurant; Charlotte's was a popular gathering spot on Friday nights after the high school football games and other sporting events. Many residents still describe Charlotte's pizza as the best-tasting thin-crust dish in northern Illinois. Its recipe for its unique pizza died with the demise of the restaurant.

The late 1980s witnessed a rise in retail store openings. Sadly, one of its most famous landmarks, Lipofsky's Department Store, was consumed by fire a week before Christmas 1989. The owner, Harold Lipofsky, and the fire department fought valiantly to save the building. Sadly, the fire flamed by wires within the building spread out of control, and the structure soon lay in waste.

As Barrington celebrates its sesquicentennial, it continues to maintain a small-town atmosphere while constantly evolving. Businesses have opened and closed, expanded and contracted. The heart of the town has undergone

Sesquicentennial "Welcome to Barrington" signs greet people driving into the village. The Lions Club provided the area with the signs.

major renovations making shopping, eating and visiting ever more pleasant, ever friendlier.

Nonetheless, concerns remain. Traffic problems persist. The purchase of the EJ&E line by Canadian National Railroad has brought a considerable amount of noise, dust and long trains through the community at all hours of the day and night. In addition, these trains contribute to the congestion of the village because now two major rail lines—the CN (Canadian National) and Metra (the former Northwestern Railroad that serves Chicago-bound commuters)—crisscross the city center.

Like communities across America, Barrington has felt the economic pinch. The village has had to lay off longtime workers and cut back services while taxes have increased—raising the ire of some. Despite the problems, many students who attended Barrington schools over the years have returned to raise their own children here. After all, Barrington is a community that cares about its neighbors and maintains its essential values: the importance of family, friends and living well.

# 2

# Churches, Schools and Cemeteries

*This country, with its institutions, belongs to the people who inhabit it.*
*—Abraham Lincoln*

Historically, churches served as the center of pioneer communities, bringing people together for friendship, companionship and spiritual enrichment. Early settlers brought with them their traditions, customs and religious affiliations. At first, services were held in homes or schools, and the preacher and faithful would arrive on horseback or in wagons pulled by oxen. When the circuit-riding preachers came to town, church members were obliged to entertain them. Families put out their best linens and tableware and served a meal fit for a Thanksgiving feast. While in the town, the country preacher also made house calls and visited the sick and shut-ins. Country churches taught the Golden Rule and the joy of being part of a family congregation. Congregants still remember and revere the life-reinforcing hymns learned at Sunday services.

As congregations grew, they raised funds to erect churches. In Barrington, two churches—one located north of today's village center and one located south of it—were established by the late 1840s. Congregationalists built the south church, but when membership declined, they sold their building to the Baptists.

Methodists, led by John Allen, moved from Dundee into Barrington. The eighteen congregants established their church in a stone schoolhouse positioned at the corners of Bateman and Algonquin Roads. When their ranks swelled to 85 members, the congregation relocated to the north church. In Cynthia Sharp's *Tales of Old Barrington*, a letter describes the church pews as "free from upholstery, free from paint, free from backs, the poorest for dozing off." Many of its pioneer parishioners are buried in the cemetery adjacent to church. With the arrival of the North Western Railroad, churchgoers wished to be more centrally located and purchased land in the village at the corners of Ela and Franklin Streets. When the thirty-four- by fifty-two-foot building was completed in 1859, it seated 125 parishioners and cost $2,200 to build. To the spartan white clapboard structure, congregants added their old church bell

Dr. Reverend James M. Wilson is the pastor of the Barrington United Methodist Church. The newly built church sits near the intersection of Routes 59 and 62 in Barrington Hills.

and enhanced the building with a sky-piercing white spire. When the group outgrew its second location, they sold the building and bought land on Cook Street. Parishioners celebrated their newest facility by adding colorful stained-glass gothic windows and a grand $500 pipe organ.

In addition to its ministerial mission, the church served as a gathering place for residents, and during the Civil War, it became a recruiting center for local men. A huge boulder stands in the churchyard with a bronze tablet containing the names of area men who fought in the Great Conflict and who signed on to the war from this church in 1860. By 1871, the year of the Great Chicago Fire, the congregation once again felt a need to expand. The new church was dedicated on December 22, 1872. Originally, the building was heated by two large drum-stoves and lighted by eighty-seven oil lamps. Later, electric lights and a modern furnace provided more suitable comforts. For the next fifty years, the Cook Street site remained a focal point of many community activities, including temperance meetings, literary gatherings, lectures and concerts, as well as a youth social center.

In 1925, plans got underway to build still another church. This time the site chosen faced Route 59 parallel to Hough Street School. That year, the church got a new pastor, Reverend H.L. Buthman. Notably charismatic and endeared by his congregation, the reverend was nicknamed "Boots." He took a leading role in raising money for the new church. In 1929, when the Great Depression hit the nation and Reverend Buthman lay in a hospital dying of cancer, plans to continue with construction were in jeopardy. From his bed, Boots told some of his closest parishioners that his wish was for the congregation to move forward with church construction. A committee of five men elected to press onward. They bought the old Zion Church and moved it, and after a local architect "declared the church sound because of its heavy oak timbers and peg construction," it was remodeled.

Now the Methodist Church was truly in the "heart of the village." Over the years, it has spawned many organizations and agencies, some of which still serve the community: Family Services of the Barrington Area, Meals on Wheels, Hospice of Northeastern Illinois (now Journey Care), CROP Walk, Barrington Giving Day and CPR training. The church experienced numerous renovations. Twice, its iconic steeple was struck by lightning and repaired. A tragedy of epic proportion occurred on October 28, 1998, when black smoke filled the village skyline and the church was destroyed by fire ignited by a spark from workers repairing the roof. Former president of the Barrington Chamber of Commerce and member of the church Carol Beese stated, "The sense of despair that followed the old building's destruction cannot be overestimated."

Almost four years later, the jubilant congregation and its dedicated pastor, Dr. James M. Wilson, moved into their new fifty-two-thousand-square-foot home at the corner of Route 59 and Algonquin Road. The spacious campus now hosts an expansive central church, a preschool, a kindergarten classroom and a community center.

Pastor James Wilson said in an interview with the *Chicago Tribune* 2002 Community Focus edition, "It's been amazing [that] even during the time of transition, we've been able to see growth. We've added to our children's ministries and we have new music groups." Church life continues to move forward as it has for decades.

Over nine hundred members attend services in the spacious facility that is now situated not too far from the original Methodist church established over 150 years ago in the lush Fox River Valley.

The Baptist Community Church is one of the oldest churches in Barrington. It began with a congregation of twenty souls who came from Dundee in 1847 and first had to decide where to meet, who their preacher would be and whether they could raise funds to construct a church. Originally, the group held meetings in the Northway School but soon took over the vacant south church. In time, they too would move into the village.

Baptist Community Church of Barrington. At Lincoln and Grove, 1859. *Photo courtesy of the Community Church.*

Their new building had tall clear-glass windows that provided plenty of light and low-back pews that were the fashion of the day. In 1891, an efficient furnace paid for by the women's organizations from funds they earned from social events and community suppers replaced their potbellied stoves. On December 16 and 17, 1884, the church celebrated its Golden Jubilee. Two of the most beloved pastors in the Baptist Community Church history are Eugene (Gene) Nyman and the current pastor, Zina Jacque.

Arnett C. Lines breaks ground at a 1966 ceremony to add a library, an office and several classrooms to the Community Church. *Photo courtesy of the Community Church of Barrington.*

Reverend Gene Nyman and his wife, Marion, moved to Barrington from Evanston, Illinois. Gene earned his bachelor of arts degree in philosophy at the University of Minnesota in 1944, followed by a bachelor of divinity degree from Bethel Theological Seminary in St. Paul in 1945. After graduation, Nyman was commissioned a chaplain in the United States Naval Reserve and served aboard the USS *Topeka*. Gene and Marion were married after he completed his military duty.

He began attending graduate school at the University of Chicago, earned his doctoral degree in 1951 and served as minister for the Community Church from 1952 to 1990. With his wife, Marion, the couple established the arts as center stage of their church and the community. The church celebrated drama, music, paintings, sculpture, wall hangings and other art forms and displayed them throughout the church, throughout the year. The charming couple and their artistic spirits created an enthusiastic and expanded membership. Gene died in 2009, Marion in 2015; their loss is deeply mourned by his adoring congregants.

Zina Jacque came to the Community Church of Barrington (CCB) in 2007 and recently celebrated her eighth anniversary as church pastor. During a party to honor Zina's tenure held at the Onion Pub Eatery in Lake Barrington, Zina, her sister and a cousin found themselves on the dance floor singing one of their favorite Supremes' songs, "Stop! In the Name of

*Left*: Reverend Eugene (Gene) Nyman. *Photo courtesy of the Community Church of Barrington.*

*Right*: Good friends Evah Lager and Marion Nyman share time to talk after enjoying a potluck supper at the Community Church.

Dr. Reverend Zina Jacque, pastor of the Community Church of Barrington.

Love." The trio brought guests to their feet and recreated sweet memories for those who grew up with the Supremes and the music of the '60s. Zina is the first African American woman to head the CCB. She obtained her doctorate from Boston University's School of Theology. After graduation, many congregations across the county sought Zina and her dynamic speaking style. Members of CCB relish the fact that she chose their church in which to make a difference, spread fellowship and with which to share her faith. The church of seventy-five families has celebrated its 175th anniversary and continues to welcome people who feel that this church, and its members, is the *right* church for them. Pastor Zina is one who truly makes that experience possible.

Settlers to Barrington were German farmers who moved here from the East Coast. They brought with them their religious traditions, hymns and language and established St. Paul's United Evangelical Church in 1863. Services were held in the German tongue well into the twentieth century, and as was the practice in Germany, men and women sat across the aisle from one another. At first, the church had no heat source; later, a wood-burning stove was installed. For a long time though, it was not unusual for the minister and the congregation to sit wearing heavy overcoats and mittens during winter services on Sunday mornings.

Willow Creek is a nondenominational mega-church located in South Barrington. Bill Hybels opened the building on October 12, 1975. He envisioned a church that would make religion relevant to a religiously disenfranchised America. In 1981, the church purchased 90 acres in South Barrington to build its campus. Today, its property covers over 155 acres and has one worship center that can accommodate seven thousand people. Total attendance of all weekend services averages twenty-five thousand attendees. According to the church philosophy, Willow Creek is "dedicated to helping irreligious people become fully devout followers of Jesus Christ."

The Willow Creek Church Sign on Highway 59 in South Barrington welcomes members and guests.

To Gene Appel, the teaching pastor, the church "isn't looking to its past; it is looking to its future." Appel said the church opens its arms to people, regardless of their social status, race, creed or type of need. Membership has exploded beyond South Barrington to across the globe. Appel believes that people are looking for answers to essential questions: Why am I here? Is there a God? What is His purpose for me? Critics may scoff at the size of the church, but Appel says, "It takes all kinds of churches to communicate with people. We're trying to reach the people God has called us to reach."

On April 27, 1932, St. Matthew Lutheran Church was chartered with a congregation of thirty-five members. In October of the following year, Reverend A.T. Kretzmann was installed as the first pastor. He also served as minister to St. John Lutheran Church in Island Lake until 1953, when he left the area to move to Trinity Lutheran Church in Crete, Illinois. The second parson at St. Matthew's was Reverend H.H. Heinemann, who was installed on April 29, 1945. Having expanded their original church at Lill and Coolidge Streets, the congregation purchased ten acres of land just outside the village limits and south of Evergreen Cemetery. The new church was dedicated on February 22, 1959. In 1971, the congregation decided to expand its facility again. Office space, classrooms, a youth center and a gymnasium were proposed. The new additions were dedicated on September 9, 1973. After serving his congregation for thirty-six years, Pastor Heinemann retired. Reverend Robert Moll replaced him and remained in that position for twenty-five years. In 2007, the church celebrated its seventy-fifth anniversary. From that time until 2012, vacancy pastors offered spiritual services at St. Matthew's. Today, this Lutheran community is led by Reverend Marc Cohen.

The Catholic Church was organized as a mission in the 1860s when traveling priests came to celebrate mass. It became know as St. Anne Church in 1884, but Catholics did not have a resident pastor until 1905. They opened St. Anne's School in 1927 under the direction of the Sisters of Mercy. Many changes came to the congregation over the next thirty years. By the 1950s, major building projects were underway. Most significant was the enlargement of the church and school. Father Thane oversaw the expansion.

Fathers Alexander Thane, Arthur Dillion and John Dewes are three of the most celebrated priests of St. Anne's parish. Father Thane served the community for twenty-eight years and witnessed the parish transform from a sleepy rural church to a vibrant suburban religious community. It was under Father Dillion's direction that St. Anne's continued to grow. While he was pastor, a new parish center and rectory were built and dedicated in 1980. The large brick facility was named in Father Dillion's honor. After fifty years of priestly duties, he died on March 2, 2004.

At the invitation of Cardinal Joseph Bernadine, Father Dewes came to St. Anne's on August 31, 1989. After shepherding the church community for twenty-two years, Dewes retired. He is best remembered for enthralling his congregants with animated tales of growing up in Oak Park, Illinois. His stories were drawn from his father's work at Illinois Bell and his mother's job as a proofreader for the *Chicago Tribune*. His parents and an uncle who lived with the family were Dewes's story-telling inspirations. Dewes attended Quigley Preparatory Seminary and was ordained after finishing his education. In 2000, the church dedicated its new and greatly enlarged facility. Father Dewes was passionate about the arts, and many art forms grace the church campus because of him. His recent retirement is bittersweet for those who hold fond memories of this dedicated priest. Today, St. Anne's supports more than three thousand households and is a vibrant member of the Barrington community.

On Easter Sunday, April 17, 1960, the picturesque, high-on-a-hill, Presbyterian Church of Barrington (PCB) on West Brinker Road was officially organized. Prior to that time, members held services in homes and at the

Father Jack Dewes shepherded St. Anne's congregation for years. He started welcome dinners for new members that enabled them to connect with seasoned parishioners. *Portrait courtesy of Thomas Balsamo.*

nearby Countryside School. In over fifty years, the church has had only four head pastors. The Reverend Mr. Paul Winchester was elected its first pastor, and he remained at the church until 1963, when he moved to Grosse Point, Michigan. After a nine-month search, the Reverend Dr. C. Victor Brown was chosen to lead the congregation. On November 7, 1965, a building committee was formed to study plans for a new Christian education wing. Groundbreaking ceremonies took place on January 8, 1967. The project was dedicated on June 9, 1968. Music is an essential component of the church. Members and guests are drawn to services by the dynamic musical offerings that include an adult sanctuary choir, a bell choir, a children's choir and a spate of guest musicians. In keeping with the times, the PCB will soon be offering live video streaming of its worship services. Currently, members and the community can receive services on their home computers. The church's website reads, "We are a close community of faith, grounded in reformed tradition, who seek to explore and understand the world we live in today through worship, service, education and lifelong learning."

Today, growth is the key to Barrington-area churches. Young families are seeking churches that provide family activities, supportive services and educational opportunities. Historically, the churches were the soul of communities, and they continue to bring people together from throughout the community.

Education builds community bridges and is a cornerstone of American life. This country has been molded by millions of immigrants who fled their homelands for political, social or religious reasons. Immigrants came here to improve their lives. They transformed the cities, the prairies and the farmlands. They believed educating their children offered them upward mobility, opportunities and the hope that they could be "all that they want to be." They understood there is no substitute for knowledge.

*Left*: Christian Science Reading Room. The church had its origin in 1910. The congregation built its stone church on East Main Street between 1924 and 1925.

*Below*: A one-room schoolhouse that has been greatly enhanced is now a family residence on South Cuba Road.

Reading and writing became a goal for the children of newcomers who also needed to learn the amount of ear corn in a crib, grain in a bin and hay in a stack. Education had to be to be pragmatic. One-room schoolhouses were commonplace—students in grades one through eight sat in the same classroom where they learned from their often young teachers as well as from one another. Rural children looked forward to the first day of school, so welcome after a summer of hard work and hot days. Children often carried bread and butter sandwiches along with a piece of fruit in their tin lunch pails.

The first known Barrington one-room schoolhouse was located at the intersection of Algonquin and Sutton Roads. It was built in 1835, and classes started that year in October. Present-day Community Unit School 220's roots began in 1840, when settlers demanded schools be available for their children. On January 9, 1841, a notice was posted stating that there would be a meeting of local parents to discuss educational needs. At the meeting it was decided to establish five school districts in different sections of the township. They included #1, to serve the eastern half (Village); #2, to serve the northwest corner; #3, to serve the west central corner; #4, to serve the southwest corner; and #5, to serve the northern area. Each district would also need elected trustees.

Contracts stated that teachers were to be "a sober person of good morals." Many were spinsters who dedicated their lives to area children. Students arrived before school and helped the teacher build a fire in the stove, collect water in a bucket and ready the classroom for lessons. Children sat many to each long row of desks that lined up facing the front of the room and the teacher. They used chalk and erasable slates to learn the alphabet, copy spelling words, compute math problems and write down pithy sayings that were to be memorized. Schools became a staple of the early communities.

By 1846, a country school was built of logs from the nearby woods on the north side of County Line Road near the present location of the Catlow Theater. In 1855, a two-story white frame school was built on the south side of Hough Street. Students who received their elementary school education in countryside, one-room schools were next sent into the village to finish their learning. Hough Street School had two wings: one on the north side taught elementary students, and one on the south side was for higher-grade pupils. In 1888, ten students earned diplomas as the first graduating class of the two-year high school. The first four-year class did not graduate until 1907.

In 1920, Barrington established a community school board when it selected Edward Riley, Arnold Sass, John Miller, Edward Walthausen and Edward Gruber to serve on the school overseeing committee. The board had six responsibilities:

- *Operate school for nine months per year.*
- *Raise enough money to operate the school.*
- *Hire a superintendent.*
- *Visit and inspect the facilities to ensure state requirements are followed.*
- *Create general policies.*
- *Report to the County Superintendent of School.*

In the mid-1940s, residents began to complain about the crowded conditions at Hough Street School. A referendum to establish a community high school was soundly defeated by a vote of 357 "yes" and 542 "no." Around this time, the board chose Dr. W.C. Reavis of the University of Chicago to prepare a comprehensive study of local educational needs and how to finance a high school. As an outcome of the study, on March 30, 1946, residents approved a high school referendum by a vote of 1,023 "yes" to 149 "no."

Following the recommendations of Reavis, the vote established Barrington Consolidated High School District 224 (BHS). It was the first high school built in Illinois after World War II. The new school set high standards for its multiple uses of space, its ideal teaching and activity facilities and for its structural design and equipment that required minimum maintenance costs. To this day, BHS is committed to its student population. Ninety-eight percent of its graduates enroll in college or post-graduate training programs. Barrington High School encourages its students to excel in academics, as well as in a variety of other programs to help them foster their talents outside the classroom. The school ranks in the top 1 percent of more than 14,350 high schools on the national level for the number of AP exams taken by its students. Its physics program was featured in a PBS documentary, and its fine arts program is one of the most comprehensive and diverse in the nation. It has won Grammy Awards and launched students into lifelong careers in the arts. Other areas of outstanding recognition include the performing arts department in the areas of music, drama and dance. Programs in foreign languages, debate, chess, scholastic bowl and video production have also earned awards and accolades.

Barrington High School was dedicated in 1949. Today, after many renovations and additions, it hosts over 2,800 students.

BHS students have been invited to perform across the country and in Europe to rave reviews. Athletic programs shine as well at BHS. Interscholastic athletic teams have won trophies and championships for basketball, baseball, golf, gymnastics, wrestling, football, soccer, badminton, bowling, tennis, cheerleading, track and field, cross country, hockey, lacrosse and poms. BHS has something to offer every student. BHS graduates have gone on to become distinguished in many fields, including, art, opera, soap opera, TV news, medicine, business, education and literature. Below is a list of Barrington's Distinguished Graduates.

## DISTINGUISHED GRADUATES OF BARRINGTON HIGH SCHOOL

| Name | Career | Year Graduated |
|------|--------|----------------|
| Harold D. Kelsey | State Government | 1918 |
| Earl M. Schwemm | Business/Community Service | 1920 |
| Foster M. Rieke | Science | 1923 |
| Ray A. Wichman | Community Service | 1928 |
| Harold Lipofsky | Community Service | 1940 |
| Dr. Jack D. Noyes | Veterinary Medicine | 1948 |
| Richard Threkeld | Communications | 1955 |
| Charles L. Mee, Jr. | Literature | 1956 |
| Marvin Lipofsky | Art - Glass blowing | 1957 |
| Stephen Ellenwood | Education | 1959 |
| Dr. Bruce Bell | Medicine/Community Service | 1959 |
| Henry M. Paulson, Jr. | Public Service/Government | 1964 |

| Name | Career | Year Graduated |
|------|--------|----------------|
| Barbara Bash | Literature | 1966 |
| Claire Bataille | Performing Arts | 1970 |
| Dr. Sarah Speck | Medicine | 1967 |
| John and Jim Feit | Community and Public Service | 1968 / 1976 |
| Jan W. Simek | Education | 1970 |
| Claire Bataille | Performing Arts | 1970 |
| John Lahey | Architect | 1971 |
| Dr. Joseph Michelotti | Medicine | 1971 |
| Dr. Bryan K. Foy | Medicine | 1971 |
| Colleen Zenk Pinter | Performing Arts | 1971 |
| Gary Fencik | Professional Athletics | 1972 |
| Corrine Wood | Public Service/Government | 1972 |
| Susan Lyons | Art/Environmental Awareness | 1972 |
| Dr. Lorena Beese | Science | 1974 |
| Dr. Carolyn Kirschner | Medicine/Community Service | 1975 |
| Deborah L. Chabrian | Art | 1976 |
| Gary Hallberg | Professional Athletics | 1976 |
| Cynthia Rowley | Fashion Design | 1976 |
| Terry Morgan | Communications | 1978 |
| Kallen Esperian | Performing Arts | 1979 |
| Michael Bergin | Science | 1982 |
| Laura Jakubec King | Humanitarian | 1983 |
| Greg Garre | Public Service/Government | 1983 |
| Donn Branstrator | Education Awareness | 1983 |
| T. R. Youngstrom | Photographer | 1984 |
| Wallace J. Nichols | Science | 1985 |
| Dan Wilson | Professional Athletics | 1987 |
| Brady Smith | Professional Athletics | 1991 |
| Veronica Roth | Literature | 2006 |

After World War II and the baby boom, more school facilities were needed across the nation. Between 1954 and 1959, District 4 added Grove Avenue and Roslyn Road Schools. Meanwhile, District 1 built Sunny Hill

Elementary and Hickory Hill Middle School. In 1947, another school was built north of the village. By the mid-1960s, old Hough Street School showed lots of wear and tear. Serious structural problems surfaced, and the building was condemned for safety violations. The school district proposed a bond referendum to build a middle school. The bond issue failed. When residents were made aware of the structural engineering concerns facing the Hough Street School's facility, a second proposed bond issue passed. Under the governance of energetic and forward-looking Superintendent Robert M. Finley, Barrington Middle School (now Station Campus) came into existence. The middle school housed students in grades six through eight and was located on Eastern (John Snow) Avenue. In January 1966, one wing of the middle school opened to sixth graders who were previously housed in the Methodist Church basement across Hough Street and in the Salem Church, south of old Hough Street School. Seventh- and eighth-grade students arrived later that spring. From its inception, the middle school shook the community with its innovative educational philosophy and unconventional programs. It was a campus "without walls," which taught "modern math," featured open-room classrooms and promoted team teaching. The nontraditional school philosophy earned a one-year Ford Foundation Grant for a "tour guide" who escorted educators from around the world wanting to learn about and see this ultra-modern facility in action.

Arnett C. Lines Elementary School opened its doors in 1969. This shell of a school opened without heat, phones or washrooms. On schedule,

*Left*: Superintendent Dr. Robert M. Finley brought numerous innovations to Barrington schools. He added team teaching, open classrooms and modern math. He had a deep regard and respect for faculty and students. *Image from Barrington School's Archives*.

*Below*: Barrington Middle School, now BMS Station Campus, opened its doors to sixth-, seventh- and eighth-grade students in 1966.

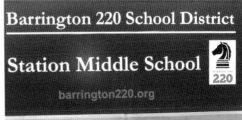

*Left*: John T. Snow became the first principal at the Arnett C. Lines School, opened in 1969. The school was named in honor of Arnett C. Lines, Barrington historian and longtime school board member.

*Right*: Jane Dawson, secretary to Snow for seventeen years, was inducted into the Barrington Senior Citizens Hall of Fame in 2010.

twice each day at ten and one o'clock, Lines children and teachers walked the "wooden planks path" between Lines School and the middle school to use its bathrooms. No one questioned the "wisdom" of the decision to open the bunker-feeling school in the fall of 1969. Teachers, students and support staff accepted these unorthodox conditions as doable. In addition to the bare stone walls and light bulbs that hung from exposed electrical wires, Lines School consisted of two staffs—sixth-grade teachers and K-5 teachers. They started and ended their days at different times and served different populations but managed to work together under the masterful guidance of Principal John T. Snow. Today, these conditions would be unthinkable—they would be illegal.

> *To speak the name of the dead is to make him live again.*
> *—Egyptian belief*

Cemeteries are silent historic landmarks. Before the twentieth century, people flocked to these "cities of the dead" on weekends, as they were located outside tenement city centers and offered people green, open spaces; fresh air; and a place to picnic where their children could play games of tag, ghost in the graveyard and collect fireflies in Mason jars at dusk. In metropolitan areas, the dead were buried on the outskirts of the cities in order to separate urban center turmoil from the solitude and quiet of the countryside. These were hallowed grounds, places to connect the living to their past and places to honor deceased members of their families. In rural areas, farmers designated part of their land to bury the dead. Across the country, many Americans are buried on back lots of farm fields.

Barrington has numerous historic grave sites where its cherished departed are buried. Barrington Center Cemetery is located on the south side of Algonquin Road and one-half mile east of Bateman Road. Farmer Henry Smith deeded 1.03 acres of his farm for the cemetery on July 5, 1866. Many graves dating from the mid- to late 1800s can be found here. Its first occupant was Jerusha Miller, wife of Seymour Miller, who died on November 7, 1840. About thirty early settlers were buried on the north side of the cemetery by 1853. The cemetery also has a plaque mounted on a large boulder at the west side of the old church that honors ninety-one Civil War soldiers. A twenty-foot easement was added in 1963. By 1979, it was reported that one hundred graves sat in the cemetery. The property is now under the jurisdiction of the Barrington Township trustees.

Cady Cemetery rests on the west side of Ela Road, one-quarter mile south of Dundee Road. It has fewer than fifty graves of many early settlers. The Cady farm once was located across the road from its present site. The cemetery is all but invisible to passengers in cars traveling along Ela and Dundee Roads.

David Haeger Cemetery rests on private property. It was set aside in 1854 by the Haeger family and named for the Haegers who settled in these parts after emigrating from Germany. The family farm was located near Spring Creek and Meadow Hill Roads. David Haeger and his son D.H. Haeger started a grain elevator and brick business in Barrington. Today, the Haeger Family is renowned for its pottery business. The factory opened operations in 1871 right after the Great Chicago Fire. The Haegers made bricks to help rebuild the ash-laden, burned-out city. Haeger Pottery business is still in operation in West Dundee, Illinois, and is known across the nation for its colorful earthenware products.

Evergreen Cemetery is the most familiar resting place to Barrington residents. It is situated immediately west of Dundee Avenue and north of Westwood Drive. It is the area's largest cemetery. George Ela, M.B. Macintosh

*Left*: Stone Monument is a tribute to four branches of the service: army, navy, air force and marines.

*Below*: Monument Road leading into Evergreen Cemetery. Flags fly for the Memorial Day Parade.

and William G. Waterman, who purchased the land from Henry Clausen, organized Evergreen between 1850 and 1855. It was chartered in 1869 and now covers more than thirty-three acres. Barrington village presidents, local legislators, well-known business figures and families, veterans and other area residents are buried here. The dedication of the grounds took place in 1906. A Civil War Monument, also called the Soldiers and Sailors Monument, is the cemetery's anchor. Three Civil War canons placed along the front of the monument's circular plot of ground are welded in place. After World War I, American Legion Post 158 purchased land west of the monument for veterans who have a Barrington address to be buried. This land was dedicated on Memorial Day 1955. Over 118 war veterans are buried at Evergreen. The VFW places American flags at their grave sites on July 4 and Veterans Day. A brightly lighted flag flies next to the Civil War statue 24/7 over the graves.

St. Paul's Cemetery is on the north side of East Main Street, just east of Route 14, and is maintained by St. Paul's United Church of Christ. Seven Civil War veterans are buried here, as well as many German

A Catlow tombstone located in Evergreen Cemetery. The Catlows are one of Barrington's most well-known families. The historic theater, in the heart of the village, in town bears the name Catlow.

*Above*: St. Paul's Cemetery is located on Main Street and was established in 1863. Many people buried at St. Paul's were German-speaking immigrants.

*Left*: White Cemetery on Cuba Road has a reputation for being haunted. To this day, no ghosts have been apprehended. Cuba Township maintains the cemetery.

families who were among the area's first settlers. Tomb inscriptions are often in German.

The White Cemetery can be found at the corner of Cuba and Barrington Roads. Cuba Township cares for the property. Among those buried here are T.W. White and Innis Hollister, two local farmers who charted the cemetery in 1855. Some believe that the cemetery is haunted. Over the years, paranormal activity has sent many "witnesses" to the local police with claims of unbelievable visions. They talk of seeing luminescent balls of light, phantom vehicles and even a vanishing house. In addition, there have been reports of the sound of leaves crushing under invisible feet and tombstones toppling for no apparent reason. The most compelling story about White Cemetery centers around a proclaimed "ghost house" that is said to have at least one resident. Eyewitnesses have reported seeing an old woman who wanders Cuba Road. She is often not alone in her wanderings. Rumors of spirits at the White Cemetery have diminished over the years, but the area is still active with the curious who relish roaming cemeteries and haunted houses on "fright-nights." Today, the cemetery is locked behind an iron fence to prevent vandalism and unwanted visitors who have plagued the site for years. In order to visit the dead who are buried at White Cemetery, the authorization of Pricilla Rose, the Cuba Township clerk, is needed to gain entry.

A community is often judged by its church attendance, the quality of its schools and its respect for the deceased members of its community. Barrington is a gold medal village when evaluated by these terms.

# 3
# *Art and Culture*

*Art is long, life short; judement diffictut; oppurtunuity transient.*
*—Goethe*

Barrington hums and buzzes with a passion for art, and its rich cultural opportunities enrich the lives of its people. Barrington is a vibrant community that offers a vast variety of venues for both art and artists. It celebrates the arts with annual open-air fairs and festivals, including Art in the Barn and Art in Nature offered at Crabtree Nature Center each fall. It includes yearly yuletide performances of *The Nutcracker*, dance shows and plays at the high school, Oscar shorts shown right before the Oscars at the legendary Catlow Theater, concerts in homes, lectures on art and opera and a broad array of art galleries for viewing and purchasing art.

Throughout Barrington District 220 schools, art remains an essential component of the curricula. Many graduates have gone on to distinguished careers in the arts locally and around the world. The range of their work includes books, movies, music, paintings, glass blowing, jewelry, documentaries and plays, caricatures and sketches, opera and soap operas, fashion, sculpture and more. The joy of community art is a source of inspiration and sustenance for the souls of Barrington citizens.

One of the primary forces behind the appreciation of art in Barrington rests with Flora (Flo) Bash, who helped establish and presided over the Barrington Area Arts Council (BAAC). With the encouragement and support of Don Klein, president of the Barrington Area Council of Governments

(BACOG), Bash established BAAC in 1976. She said of her mission, "BAAC is a group of citizens charged with the need to stimulate more participation in the arts on a local level." A diminutive woman with a dynamic personality, Bash promoted creativity in the literary, graphic and performing arts. During World War II, she was a writer and producer of musical radio shows in Chicago. When the Bash family moved to Barrington Hills, Flo brought her love of the arts with her. For three decades, she was the guiding spirit behind many of Barrington's cultural events.

Among BAAC's principal accomplishments were the annual Young Writers Project, BAAC Art Gallery, Library Sculpture Garden, Summer Art Fair (and Run for the Arts), the Walter A. Horban Classical Music Scholarship Competition and the Barrington Writers Workshop, which continues to this day.

One of BAAC's first projects was to establish an art gallery in the Barrington Area Library. Bash considered books and art a spiritual pairing. When she opened the gallery, she invited Barrington High School faculty members to contribute their art for the opening show. The council's first home was established in the former United Methodist Church on Hough Street in October 1982. Later, the council moved to a storefront building on Main Street and later to a more spacious and handsome gallery on Park Avenue, where it operated for almost two decades.

Bash nurtured and promoted the talents of artists from all over the world and helped open the eyes of Barrington's citizens to international art as well as art in their own backyard. She was "the wind beneath the wings" of many area artists. In May 1977, Bash brought an International Folk Festival to Barrington Middle School. The evening featured folk dancers and music from Spain, Latin America, Greece, Russia, Lithuania and the Philippines. It won great acclaim from the community, which clamored for more of these events. In 1982, Bash helped launch *Whetstone*, an award-winning, soft-covered yearly publication of original fiction, creative nonfiction and poetry; *Whetstone*'s purpose was to highlight established and emerging writers. The fifteenth volume of *Whetstone* was dedicated to Flo Bash "in celebration of [her] vision and enthusiasm." Bash was a staunch advocate of the arts and culture in the Barrington area, where her legacy lives on.

Kathy Umlauf, one of the original members of BAAC, went on to inaugurate the Northwest Cultural Council (NWCC) in September 1988. The council's goal was to be a supportive expression of creative people living in Barrington and the surrounding communities. Umlauf, raised in

The logo for the former Barrington Area Arts Council, which promoted the arts throughout the year, throughout the community.

Chicago, carried her zeal for the arts to Deer Park where she and her husband, David, live.

As executive director of NWCC, Umlauf's first project was to usher in a quarterly newsletter, *SPOTLIGHTS*, to feature a calendar of community cultural events, photos and articles about art and artists. Through an ongoing generous contribution, Northrop Grumman has published *SPOTLIGHTS* for NWCC for the past twenty-six years. Each issue is a work of art on its own terms.

Umlauf next formed the Corporate Galleries, an association of local businesses and libraries. According to Umlauf, "They enable artists who exhibit exceptional credentials and talent, who contribute to the Council's commitment to excellence, in a space to celebrate their art." Exhibitions change regularly. NWCC allows a variety of artists to place their work for public viewing. Between twenty and thirty professionally juried artists offer works, which include sculpture, photography, wearable art, embroideries, crocheted pieces, quilts, tapestries, ceramics, pencil drawings, mixed media and oil, acrylic and water color paintings.

Another highly regarded program initiated by Umlauf is Kids Meet Art™. The children's art-education program started at Fremd High School in Palatine. It spread through the northwest corridor, serving students from kindergarten through high school. According to Umlauf, the goal of her 1995 Kids Meet Art™ program is to provide students with art that they have never experienced before—whether it is writing a haiku, hearing a bagpiper, learning to draw in perspective or creating paper collages. The program has been underwritten with grants from individuals and corporations that understand the importance of bringing art to students who might never have the opportunity to see or participate in artistic experiences. This cause has become even more important in this budget-conscious age; school funding is being cut, forcing schools to eliminate art and music.

In 2001, with the assistance of poet Deborah Nodler Rosen, editor of the acclaimed Chicagoland poetry magazine *Rhino*, NWCC put on a monthly workshop led by published poets. The program started with a handful of

*Left*: The logo for Northwest Cultural Council, which promotes all the arts for everyone from youngsters to adults.

*Middle*: David Hill was a dedicated supporter of the arts. He provided the NWCC with a spacious office and gallery for years.

*Bottom*: Deborah Nodler Rosen and Kathy Umlauf, executive director of the Northwest Cultural Council, discuss a new art installation on display at the Corporate Gallery.

participants and has burgeoned into a group of regulars who have honed their craft under the tutelage of group instructors. As a result, many have become published poets. Their works appear in magazines, in chapbooks, on the Internet and even on overhead posters on public transportation across the country. The Second Saturday Poets have read their works for several years at Deer Park's Barnes & Noble during April's Poetry Month, at the Palatine Public Library, at the Arlington Green Executive Center and at Loyola University's Cunco Mansion and Gardens in Vernon Hills. There they launched their first chapbook, featuring the poetry of workshop leaders and participants as well as images by gallery artists. The chapbook resulted in a unique marriage of oral and visual creativity.

Two men who have had an enormous impact on the NWCC are the late David Hill and Martin Ryan. Martin chaired the Fine Arts Department at Harper College and was one of the founding members of NWCC. He served as editor of prose and poetry for *SPOTLIGHTS*. Ryan, an advocate of introducing young people to poetry, held poetry-reading sessions at the Kimball Hill gallery for Rolling Meadows High School students. A distinguished poet in his own right, in 2003, he published *Destinations*, a handsome book of his poems that covered decades of work.

David Hill was president of Kimball Hill Homes and an avid supporter of the arts. He provided a spacious home and gallery for NWCC at his corporate office. The venue hosted art exhibits, workshops and conferences for many years. Hill also enjoyed the arts, and he often was seen reading books and enchanting schoolchildren.

Ed Walaitis was born in Bayonne, New Jersey. As an infant, he went with his mother to visit her native Lithuania. Mother and child were stranded in the Baltic state due to the outbreak of World War I. They stayed for many years after the conflict ended, and Walaitis used the time to attend school. Walaitis returned to the States when he was sixteen. The self-taught watercolorist learned to draw while creating layouts for several New York City advertising firms and Macy's Department Store.

In the early 1940s, Walaitis moved to Chicago and worked as a freelancer and artist for Montgomery Ward. In 1945, he married his wife, Marcia, also an artist. Later, he took a job with the *Chicago Tribune* in the advertising art department and became its director. His watercolors drew national attention, and he received many awards from such organizations as the Union League Club of Chicago, the Artists Guild of Chicago, the Springfield (Missouri) Museum and many others. Collectors of Walaitis's works include the Honeywell Corporation and the Ford Motor Company. His works appeared in several national publications, including *Newsweek*, *Ford Times* and *Yankee Magazine* and was often featured in the *Chicago Tribune*. Walaitis moved to Barrington, which became the inspiration of many of his works. He was known for his Chicago cityscapes, carousel horses and Canada geese. He died of natural causes at the age of ninety-one while living in Florida.

Life is frequently ordered and shaped by unfortunate events. Shortly after World War II, polio wasn't just another disease; it became every parent's worst nightmare. There was no place to escape from the crippling malady; children and adults were equally at its mercy. When Charles Mee Jr. was fifteen and a freshman at Barrington High School, his aspiration was to play football at Notre Dame University.

In the summer of 1953, one year before massive testing of the Salk polio vaccine, Mee was attending a party with some of his friends at Barrington Hills Country Club. The night included dinner, dancing and a swim in the club's pool. As night began to fall, Mee felt weak in the knees; they felt rubbery, and he could hardly stand. In his book *A Nearly Normal Life*, Mee describes that night as the beginning of his polio ordeal. "Going for a swim was out of the question. To think of it made me shiver. Fear had begun to overtake me—deep down…danger signals were going off, telling me that this was not a previous sort of sickness—but I fought it off."

The double-dating foursome left the club and headed for his date, Stevie's, house and to the "safety" of the downstairs rec room. Mee wasn't feeling any better. After awhile, he crawled up the basement stairs and across several nearby lawns to his home. Trying not to alarm his parents, Mee moved as quietly as he could, but he stumbled up the stairs toward his bedroom and moved about the hallway to ease the agony in his legs. When his parents heard the commotion, they went to investigate. Quickly realizing the gravity of his situation and after they consulted with a local doctor, they rushed Charles by car to the closest hospital, Sherman, in Elgin. A nurse took one look at the boy in a wheelchair and pronounced: "This boy has polio." Everyone backed away, running to scrub their skin's surfaces, knowing that the highly contagious disease might cause their own paralysis or death.

In the isolation ward—or "lonely ward," as Mee called it—he went from being a healthy, athletic boy to a frightened child of merely ninety pounds who could only move three fingers on his left hand. Months later and with intense physical therapy Mee was able to return home and eventually attend school on crutches. During his confinement, he had learned to love reading and appreciate four special Barrington teachers who supplied him with interesting reads and encouragement: Maude Strouss, Grace Wandke, Annette Scheel and Alan Peshkin.

After high school, Mee entered Harvard to study history and literature. He graduated in 1960 and moved to Greenwich Village. He knew he needed an occupation that would allow him to sit down while on the job—so he began writing plays. Of his life today, he says: "I begin every morning with a cup of tea and I disappear into a tiny room off the kitchen to work. My days are just incredibly boring—and I love them."

Mee's plays have received lavish praise and honors: a lifetime achievement award from the American Academy of Arts and Letters, two OBIE Awards, a PEN/Laura Pels Award for Drama and the Fisher Award of the Brooklyn Academy of Music. He describes his works as "broken, jagged and filled with sharp edges. It feels like my life. It feels like the world."

Charles Mee has four grown children and lives with his wife in Brooklyn. He still uses a cane or canes to steady his feet, but he journeys onward, remembering a time when he was not able to move more than a few fingers.

Vince Lombardo grew up along Hope Street near Chicago's Loop. The Northwestside community was pressed between Taylor and Halsted Streets and was an ethnically diverse environment where many Italian immigrants settled. It is the place that fostered Vince's imagination with vivid and abundant lasting impressions.

Lombardo was born in Chicago on October 25, 1927. He often remarked that the family's house with seven people could fit into the living room of his Barrington home. Vince served as a clerk for the army air corps stateside during World War II. The young boy remembers being motivated by his third-grade teacher, who recognized his word wisdom, to keep a notebook of his poems and stories. Vince followed her lead. As he grew older, he wrote about his neighbors: the Polopoulos family who lived across the street, the Barcias who lived two doors down and countless Italian families who journeyed to Hope Street from Bari, Naples and Sicily. His paternal family was Sicilian. Lombardo gathered the sights, sounds and smells of his village and began writing their stories. Lombardo graduated with a master's degree in education from the University of Illinois in Urbana-Champaign in 1953. Vince married his sweetheart, Therese Rose, on July 25, 1953. The couple have three daughters, Elizabeth, Laura and Mary, and two sons, Phillip and John. Three months after graduation, Lombardo became a Spanish teacher at BHS. His charges fell in love with this suave, always-smiling man who often greeting them at the door of his classroom singing in Spanish or

Italian. Students who entered his room felt certain magic attracting them to Lombardo's style. Being assigned to his Spanish class brought joy to those who were scheduled for his classes. He taught by the storytelling method, which pleased his students and made their lessons memorable. As one former student said, "I may have forgotten a lot of Spanish, because I don't use it enough, but I will never forget Señor Lombardo."

In the summer of 1982, Lombardo participated in the New Jersey Writing Project sponsored by District 220 to promote writing for teachers at every grade level. This program enabled Vince to go public with the stories he had been writing for years—stories that he had heard from his mother and father, grandfather, cousins and neighbors. He wanted to leave his works for his children and grandchildren.

By the time Lombardo was sixty-seven, he had penned three memoirs, which included tales of the Depression, glimpses into the troubles and triumphs of immigrants struggling to raise their children in a foreign land and quirky details about his own family history.

Lombardo retired from teaching in 1990, but he never lost his passion for the classroom or his love of writing. He volunteered to teach creative writing to young students from Hough Street School for several years and helped develop many a budding poet.

With the encouragement of members of the Barrington Writers Workshop, Vince began submitting his pieces for publication. His stories were seen often in *Whetstone*, the BAAC prize-winning literary magazine. Vince's story "Blood Sausage" was selected for the tenth anniversary of the publication. BAAC sent the story on to the Illinois Arts Council for its consideration, and it won first prize as an outstanding piece of creative nonfiction. Vince and BAAC were award a monetary prize for the work.

At the encouragement of fellow poets Jim Littwin, Helen Reed and Vicki Vietti, Vince published two poetry chapbooks: *Penny Waffles* and *Collected Poems*. Vince Lombardo died of cancer on June 18, 1998. A funeral mass was held at St. Anne Catholic Church, where a large crowd of former students, colleagues, neighbors, friends and family attended the June 23 service.

Following is an excerpt from Vince's short story "A Basket of Oranges":

> *On summer nights, long ago, when air conditioning was unknown except for the movie houses in the Loop, neighbors of Hope Street escaped the stifling heat captured in their houses to sit on front steps or porches. Hope Street would be filled with the murmur of voices, a Babel of different languages: Greek from the Polopoulos family across the street, Spanish*

*from the Garcia family two doors down, three to four dialects from Barese, Neapolitans and Sicilians.*

*Pushcart vendors sold ice cream, popcorn, syrup-flavored ices and most popular of all pasatempi—sand-roasted* ceci *(chick peas), bitter lupine seeds, salted squash seeds and pine nuts. On some nights, a tall, red-faced man dressed in white baker's clothes and carryng a small wash tub on his head, walked down the middle of Hope Street shouting, Cu mangi non mori mai. He who eats will never die. He sold thick bread pizzas with tomato, cheese and olive oil topping. His cry fascinated me in spite of the derisive laughter from adults.*

Stan Young was an artist known throughout the Midwest for his muted watercolors and acrylics. He was born in Edgerton, Wisconsin, on May 20, 1918, and raised in Rockford, Illinois. As a child, he was always drawing but never dreamed he could become a full-time paid artist. Young took drawing and layout classes at Rockford College and, on Saturdays, attended the American Academy of Art in Chicago. He served in World War II as a pontoon builder. His daughter, Susan Parks, recounts the time that her dad "almost died when a truck loaded with bayonets tipped over and fell on him." Soldiers lifted the truck and pulled Young from beneath the vehicle.

An Amish farmer sits atop his wagon and guides two of his horses into the family barn. *Courtesy of Susan Young Parks.*

Two Navajos survey their flock of desert sheep on the open mesa. *Courtesy of Susan Young Parks.*

Young moved to Barrington in 1958. His commercial art career was spent working at the *Des Moines Register*, United Airlines, the *Tribune* and a number of Chicago studios and ad agencies. After surviving a heart attack, Young left the stress-filled world of commercial art and "never looked back." He began taking watercolor lessons from Lou Taylor, embracing the genre and developing his skills to create fine art. He focused on landscapes of Door County, Washington Island and Lake Geneva. He filled his paintings with lively scenes of people, including Native Americans, and scenes of America and animals—especially ducks, geese and horses. Young often painted to the sounds of his favorite kinds of music: jazz and classical. When he found a scene he wanted to paint, he made sketches and took pictures of it. He preferred to paint in his studio instead of the outdoors, where insects could "get in the way." Today, his works enhance the walls of hospitals, businesses, civic buildings and private homes. "If my work can enrich someone's life, I am pleased," Young said.

Frank (Pancho) Willmarth, native son of Barrington, sketched the rich and famous and the not-so-rich-or-famous. Many of his works hung on the walls of the fabled Brown Derby in Hollywood. At a recent auction in Dallas, his caricature of President Ronald Reagan fetched $5,437. Other well-known Willmarth political portraits include Hubert Humphrey and Richard Nixon. He also sketched members of Hollywood's elite, such as Bob Hope, Cecil B.

DeMille and George Raft. Upon seeing Willmarth's sketch, Raft, dissatisfied with his image, tore up the picture but left the ribbons of paper behind. With a smile on his face, Willmarth taped the torn-up pieces back together.

Willmarth earned his living at fairs throughout the nation. He charged five dollars per picture and estimated that he had sketched at least fifty thousand portraits during his career. Art was his bread and butter, and literally, it enabled Willmarth to keep food on the family's table.

Marvin Lipofsky has been on a worldwide glass odyssey since he was first introduced to its mystical magic while studying art at the University of Wisconsin in Madison. "Glass found me," says Lipofsky, an acclaimed glass master whose works have been described as "colorful, ephemeral bubbles." He was born on September 1, 1938, to Henry and Mildred Lipofsky, a Jewish retailing family. His grandfather started the fabled Lipofsky's department store in Barrington, which was run by family members for decades.

Marvin gravitated toward art while a student at Barrington High School. After BHS, he attended the University of Illinois and graduated with a BFA in 1962. After school, he traveled to Europe and visited Murano glass factories, but it was not until later that he became intrigued by the possibilities of working with glass. In the fall of 1962, Lipofsky continued his art education at the University of Wisconsin–Madison, concentrating on sculpture. The first day of his ceramics class, he met Professor Harvey Littleton, who was just starting to organize students to blow glass. Lipofsky experimented with glass throughout his time in graduate school but maintained his interest in ceramic sculpture. He created important works such as *Tombstones*—politically inscribed ceramic slabs—and his reputation as an artist exploded. He received numerous awards for his art pieces.

In 1964, Lipofsky gained his MS and MFA in sculpture. The first job opportunity was to teach glass blowing at UC–Berkley, and he accepted. That fall, at twenty-six, he moved to California to become part of the Berkley faculty. In 1967, he established a glass program at the California College of Arts and Crafts, where he continued to teach until 1987. Lipofsky said, "My teaching style was confrontational in some respects; I want to confront [the students] not only with problems, but with ideas. My goal was not to explain everything from A to Z, but to encourage them to do their own research and discovery."

During the next several decades, he pushed the limits of working with glass in unorthodox ways while traveling as guest artist and lecturer to glass studios, schools and factories in Europe, Asia and across the United States. In 1968, he organized the First Great California Glass Symposium (an educational

Marvin Lipofsky in his studio with a fellow glass blower working on a piece called *Toso*. *Photo courtesy of Marvin Lipofsky.*

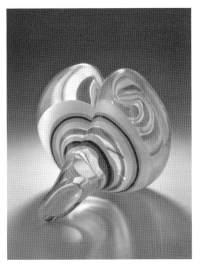 

*Left*: Lipofsky's *Fratelli 76_2*. *Photo courtesy of Marvin Lipofsky.*

*Right*: From Lipofsky's Tombstone series. *Tombstone 63_5. Photo courtesy of Marvin Lipofsky.*

exchange) that continued for two decades, hosting 105 events and ninety-eight artists. After his formal teaching career ended in 1987, he continued to be active in the glass arts community, creating his own art, giving demonstrations and lectures and as a visiting artist. He created several series—*California Loop*, *Great American Food* and *IGS Series* (created at symposiums in the Czech Republic). He is the recipient of a National Endowment for the Arts Fellowship, co-founded the Glass Arts Society and was the first editor of its journal.

Lipofsky has worked and taught in more than thirty factories, twenty-five schools and numerous hot shop studios in twenty-one countries over the past fifty years, earning him the title Roving Ambassador of Glass. His imaginative techniques with glass have influenced artists in other fields as well. Today, Lipofsky is admired as a teacher, a global ambassador and an artist with a fresh perspective. His work is truly unique and evocative.

Barbara Bash grew up in Barrington and is the daughter of Phil and Flo Bash. She graduated from BHS in 1966. Bash has lived in California and Colorado and now lives with her family on a farm in Upstate New York. She has written a series of vivid and informative book for the Sierra Club, including *Desert Giants: The Saguaro Cactus*; *Tree of Life*, which she dedicated to her BHS social studies teacher, Annette Sheel; and *A Naturalists' Guide to the Southern Rocky Mountains*. Bash began attending Audubon meetings to learn more about birds making their homes in cities. "She quickly discovered a variety of birds who had adapted to life in the city after their own natural habitats had been destroyed." Publishers print Bash's books for children, but Bash targets her books for any age group, for anyone with a passion for animals, art and city environments. In 1996, *Booklist* described Bash's book *In the Heart of the Village: The Banyan Tree* "as luminous double-spread watercolor pages. They show the tree from sunrise to sunset, as a place for meeting, nesting, giggling" and the center of life for those who live near the Banyan. "Children familiar with Bash's previous books will not be disappointed in this one." Barbara Bash is an artistic treasure whose art and richly colored books will not be soon forgotten.

Patricia Reeve Mead has been a resident of Barrington since 1970. She earned an art degree from Cornell College in Iowa that led to a fifteen-year career in graphic design in Chicago. She returned to watercolor after her retirement from commercial art; she studied at the Art Institute and the American Academy of Art in Chicago. Her works hang in public and private collections throughout the country. She is currently teaching adult watercolor classes at the Kaleidoscope School of Art in Barrington. Mead is a signature member of not only the American Watercolor Society but also the Transparent Watercolor Society of America. Her other passion is music, in particular singing and playing the piano. She has been a member of the Chicago Master Singers for over two decades and, additionally, supports them by donating her art for the group's fundraisers.

Debbie Chabrian graduated from Barrington High School in 1976. After graduation, she studied at Northern Illinois University and the Chicago Art Institute of Visual Arts, eventually moving on to the Parson's School of Design in New York City in 1980. Art has been a way of life for Chabrian, who has won many prizes and awards, starting at age eleven. As quoted in *Profiles in Excellence* from District 220, she says, "My teacher, Peggy Cullen, had great faith in me since I was a freshman." Cambrian continued, "The whole Art Department at BHS, headed by Clair Smith, was a wonderful, creative refuge for me. I appreciated BHS's Art Department even more when I went on to Parson's and found out just how well they [the teachers at BHS] had prepared me." Since leaving Barrington, Cambrian has amassed a trunk full of awards for her illustrations and watercolors. These include numerous certificates of merit from the Society of Illustrators in New York City as well as the prestigious National Galleries Endowment Award and the National Portrait Galleries Annual Exhibition Award.

Barrington-based portrait photographer Thomas Balsamo received his first camera as a gift when he was ten. His love of photography grew into a career when his parents let him set up a darkroom in their Lake Barrington basement. When he was twelve, he started a lawn-mowing business to save enough money to set up his first darkroom. When he was eighteen and a junior at BHS, he set up a studio in his parents' basement and started creating portraits.

Thomas Balsamo is rarely in front of a camera. To quote Reverend Jeannie Hanson, "Thomas looks with his eyes [at his subjects] but sees with his soul." Here, Thomas's soul shines. *Photo courtesy of Thomas Balsamo.*

For decades, his objective has been to capture a glimpse into the souls of his subjects through their eyes. He looks at each assignment as an opportunity to create art, striving to capture each person's inner self, the person's life-force. Balsamo says, "I have been compelled to create images that capture the true essence of the human spirit, rather than record only [their] physical attributes."

This goal is the core of his being for any project he takes on. CNN, CBS, WGN and WLS have featured his work. His portraits appeared in magazines such as *Professional Photographer, RangeFinder, Time, Quintessential Barrington* and *Parent*, to name a few. His portraits have received national and international acclaim. Balsamo broke ground with the publication of his books *Souls: Beneath and Beyond Autism*, published by McGraw Hill, and *I Have a Voice*. He co-authored *Souls* with Sharon Rosenbloom whose son, Joey, is autistic. The book's opening page states that this is "a project committed to portraying autism and more profoundly, individuals with autism, from the inside out." In addition, "the greater purpose…is [to learn] the universal message that, from the depths of darkness, often we find the greatest enlightenment." Balsamo's *Souls* got the attention of Toys "R" Us's philanthropic fundraising organization. He was invited to participate in joint fundraising efforts for Autism Speaks. His portraits of individuals with autism were displayed for four years in eight hundred stores across the nation and helped raise $6.5 million for Autism Speaks. Thomas Balsamo hopes *I Have a Voice* inspires readers to look at individuals with disabilities from a different light. Balsamo says, "Don't just look, see [them]. See beneath the surface beyond the diagnosis. Open your eyes to [their] boundless potential. And [their] infinite capacity to love…See deeply. Listen closely. Know them. And you will be touched forever."

In 2005, the Barrington Area Arts Council and the Barrington Area Council on Aging, along with a grant from the Illinois Arts Council, saw to the publication of Balsamo's booklet *Lives with Passion*. His collection of thirty-nine black-and-white portraits featured mature local citizens whose careers are driven by their fervor; through them, he explores dance, music, watercolors, wearable art, basket making, conservation, teaching, volunteerism, law and philanthropy. It is a celebration of the creative spirit that resides in each of us. In 2011, Thomas embarked on another project: "Express Yourself." This time, he gave special-needs students a camera and asked them to take photos of things that they love, things they can't live without, things that make them cry or laugh and things that are beautiful. With the help of local photographers, these young people were able to express their emotions in vivid detail, taking pictures of Harry Potter books ("I love the Harry Potter stories," said Bridget Duffy) or the American flag ("I think the U.S. flag is amazing. When I see the flag or hear a song about our country, I always get the 'good chills,'" remarked Kennedy Norman), and Timothy Price photographed his Legos ("I kind of like Legos. Actually I love Legos…I make up mini-figures and I put

Pat Mead, watercolorist and musician, now teaches art at the Kaleidoscope School of Art on Main Street. *Photo courtesy of Thomas Balsamo.*

John Snow, graduate of the Art Institute of Chicago, has been applying his talents using a variety of media. *Photo courtesy of Thomas Balsamo.*

Barbara Papamarcos, avid gardener and basket maker, loved both avocations with a passion and encouraged others to find their passions. *Photo courtesy of Thomas Balsamo.*

them in a scene. It is kind of neat.") Thomas's work gets the most out of his subjects no matter their age, occupation or disposition. He truly exemplifies the *art* of photography.

Recently, Balsamo joined forces with his son, Wade, in making videos and documentaries for Thomas's company called World Touch Productions. In an article in the December 2013 *Barrington Suburban Life*, Balsamo said, "Wade is really talented with audio and editing. I love working with him. We have a great synergy together." Balsamo hopes to inspire others to find and use their gifts and talents to influence good in the world.

Opera fans line up for blocks for tickets when Kallen Esperian is performing. The famous star has graced the greatest opera stages around the world. Esperian has also appeared with legendary superstars Luciano Pavarotti and Placido Domingo on numerous PBS specials.

After graduating from BHS in 1979, Esperian earned her music degree from the University of Illinois. She went on to win the coveted Luciano Pavarotti International Voice Competition in 1985, and she made her debut as Mimi in *La Boehme* in 1986 in Philadelphia. She is best known for her work in Verdi operas, which are demanding both vocally and dramatically. Critics heap praise on her brilliant performances. In 1991, Esperian appeared at Lincoln Center with Pavarotti in his annual concert and again in 1995 at

Opera star Kallen Esperian came to Deer Park Shopping Center to sign copies of her latest CD and meet with friends and fans from the Barrington area.

the Royal Albert Hall in London. The two collaborated on a CD and video entitled *Pavarotti Plus*. Esperian has shared her powerful voice and energy on numerous occasions at Chicago's Lyric Opera House and Carnegie Hall. On stage, she is a force to be reckoned with. Appearing recently at the Lyric in *Falstaff*, Esperian commented, "It's rare when you get a group of people together, in a cast of this size, where everyone is so talented and gets along so well. It's really been one of the highlights of my singing career." Beyond the operatic stage, Esperian has recorded a CD of rock and jazz classics, including a cover of "Immigrant Song" by Led Zeppelin. She now makes her home in the South.

Imagine making a film about crossword puzzles. Exciting, right? Most people would answer a definitive, "No." But that is exactly what filmmakers Patrick Creadon and Christine O'Malley decided to document. O'Malley grew up in Barrington and produced the film while her husband, Creadon, directed it. It wasn't packed with high-speed car chases, violent gun sequences or risqué bedroom dramas. The couple's movie debuted at the Sundance Film Festival. Once people set aside their skepticism, the documentary about crossword puzzles quickly became a favorite of film critics and audiences.

O'Malley began her foray into film at Barrington High School, shooting with a big, bulky video camera. At DePaul University, she majored in communication and wasn't sure what she "wanted to do with the rest of her life." She transferred to the legendary Columbia College located across the street from the Art Institute of Chicago. During the summer of 1994, O'Malley worked in Michigan on *Straight to the Heart*, a film that never saw an audience. "But, it was a great learning experience," she remembers. After college, O'Malley headed to Los Angeles. Like all aspiring movie producers, her career moved in an unexpected direction—she became a prop master. "That was good training for a producer," she said. And it was on that set where she met her future husband. After getting married, they formed their own documentary film company: O'Malley Creadon Productions. Both share a love of *New York Times* crossword puzzles. They decided that the puzzle editor, Will Short, would be the perfect subject for a film. Short agreed to the idea of creating a documentary about the annual crossword puzzle tournament. He encouraged O'Malley and Creadon to attend one of the events. "It turned out to be one of the most exciting tournaments," said O'Malley.

The film became not just a profile of Short but also examined the world of crosswords: gamers, showcasing how the puzzles are created, who works them and the daily challenges wordsmiths face to complete the puzzles. The tournament's audience contained a diverse array of notables, including former president Bill Clinton; former *Daily Show* host, Jon Stewart; documentary filmmaker Ken Burns; and the Indigo Girls—a fascinating group for a fascinating film. What will O'Malley and Creadon feature in their next film? Only time and inspiration will tell.

The BHS Distinguished Graduate Committee selected Veronica Roth as its choice for 2015. The world-acclaimed science fiction writer is the author of the highly popular *Divergent* trilogy. Hosted by the Barrington 220 Educational Foundation (seen in Chapter 8), Roth recently returned to Barrington to make several appearances. She wowed her audiences at Prairie Middle School at the BHS Black Box Theater and at a public program hosted by Barrington Middle School Station Campus. Students and adults eagerly purchased books signed by Roth. Her books *Divergent* (2001) and *Insurgent* (2012) were sold to Summit Entertainment for film rights in no time and have already reached the box office. Roth's third book, *Allegiant*, came out in 2014. Another movie is in the works. Roth reminded students that failure can be a positive motivating force as she revealed the personal challenges she faced before landing on the New York Times Best Sellers List.

After Roth graduated from Barrington High School, she went to Carleton College for one year before transferring to Northwestern University. There she enrolled in additional creative writing classes. It was at Northwestern that Roth penned her first book; she was twenty-one. A popular quote from *Divergent* is "We believe in ordinary acts of bravery, in courage that drives one person to stand up for another." Roth graduated from the university's prestigious writing program in 2010 and continued her writing career with other books and short stories.

Goodbooks Favorite Book Category selected *Divergent* as its 2011 winner. The book also earned the Best Young Adult Fantasy pick for 2012. In an interview in *Barrington Suburban Life*, Prairie seventh graders Claire Buckley and Elizabeth Leese said, "Roth's book are a quick read, easy to understand and hard to put down"—an undeniable tribute to the work of any author, rare words for one so young, so talented.

# 4

# *Sports and Recreation*

*Talent wins games, but teamwork and intelligence wins championships.*
*—Michael Jordan*

Chicago is a rabid sports city. Chicagoans cherish and lend complete allegiance to their teams: the Cubs, White Sox, Black Hawks, Bulls, Bears and Fire. They support their teams—win or lose. At the end of each sport's season, the echo of "Wait 'til next year" is heard around watering holes throughout the city. Sometimes Chicago fans wait for decades, or so it seems, for one of their teams to be champions of its league.

Gary Fencik, Walter Payton, Mike Singletary, Danny Wilson and Gary Hallberg have put Barrington on the national sports' map with their athleticism. Their skills, talents and intelligence are known around the country and have given Barrington a reputation for being the best of the best.

Legendary Chicago Bears football coach Mike Ditka told members of the 1982 squad that he would take them to the Super Bowl and win it. Ditka's prophecy came true, but it took the coach three years to fulfill his promise. Three members of the Bears team were living in Barrington at the time the club became champs: Fencik, Payton and Singletary. The community rallied behind its "men." These neighbors were often seen in and around Barrington in the stores, at the schools and watching sporting events.

The 1985 Chicago Bears football team united Chicago—a truly diverse city characterized by steel mills and the Magnificent Mile, the Pullman

Barrington High School stadium, home of the Broncos, where many a championship team played over the course of its long history.

District and Lincoln Park, the Art Institute and Hyde Park. The '85 Bears vaporized all city divisions, and Chicagoans rallied behind their "men in blue and orange jerseys."

Gary Fencik was born in Chicago on June 11, 1954, to John and Adeline. He grew up in Zion, Illinois, with five brothers and sisters and moved to Barrington in his sophomore year when his father took an administrative job at BHS. Fencik says, "I think the [Barrington] family environment helps you a lot." At BHS, Gary played basketball and football. He remembers, "From the time I was a little kid, I had a basketball in my hands. Sometimes it's nice to get into an environment like playing football, where you get to show some other side of your personality." Football endeared itself to Fencik, who was an all-conference flanker at BHS.

After graduation, Fencik had a tough decision to make: should he go to the University of Wisconsin on a football scholarship or should he go to study history at Yale? Fencik's parents always stressed academics with their children, but a full ride to Wisconsin surely had a powerful draw for a kid who excelled in sports. Fencik knew that his decision would be life altering. He said, "I always felt that education was more important than athletics." It was understandable then that Yale was his choice.

Happily, Fencik also learned that he could play football for coach Carmen Cozza at Yale. Now, he could have the best of both worlds. During his days at the Ivy League school, Fencik became an academic scholar and an athletic star as a defensive safety, a position he had once played at BHS.

Upon earning his bachelor's degree, Fencik was drafted by the Miami Dolphins. The team was peppered with veterans in the defensive position. After Fencik was injured, the Dolphins released him. The Bears picked up his contract in 1976. His first year was spent on the sidelines. His break came in 1977 after safety Doug Plank hurt his knee and was forced to sit out for three games.

Fencik's size complemented the safety position: he was six-one and weighed 160 pounds. Fencik served the Bears well during his time with the club—he was named to three NFL all-pro teams. Sports commentators remarked, "His job requires him to be fast enough to keep pace with wide receivers on pass patterns yet strong enough to ward off mammoth blockers on running plays."

Gary Fencik returned to Barrington to speak before a sold-out audience for the Educational Foundation Program. The former Bear now works and lives with his family in Chicago.

Gary Fencik was named to the Barrington High School list of Distinguished Graduates representing the class of 1972. He is recognized as a notable athlete, scholar and successful businessman. Since 1995, he has worked at Adams Street Partners—a company that specializes in the type of trading that measures returns in billions. Fencik is currently a partner and head of business development with the firm. Looking back on his career with the Bears, Fencik recently commented, "I still have fun, but nothing will ever replace the excitement of football." After his experiences with friends at Yale who were moving on to law or medical school, business or entrepreneurships, Fencik knew that if he made it to the NFL pros, there would need to be life after pros. With this in mind, in 1981, he enrolled at Northwestern's Kellogg School of Management. When the Bears made their run to a championship, he spent two nights a week studying finance. Says Fencik, "Eighty-five was good. I completed my MBA, we won the Super Bowl and I met my wife." Gary and Sandy live in Chicago and have a son and a daughter, both in college.

Bill Rose, former owner of Mill Rose Restaurant and CEO of the Rose Packing Company, lured Walter Payton to South Barrington in 1985. During his time with Ditka's Bears, Payton was the area's most famous resident. He was frequently seen at his children's sporting events.

Payton was born on July 25, 1954, in Columbus, Mississippi. He was the youngest of three children. He attended Columbia High School, where he first played football. His parents discouraged him from playing football, fearing for his safety. But Payton excelled at the sport even at a young age. At Columbia, he set the NCAA record for the most points scored, totaling 464. This too is where Payton earned the nickname Sweetness, a moniker that remained with him during his entire football career and life. After high school, Payton went to Jackson State College and graduated in three and a half years.

The Chicago Bears drafted Payton in 1975 as the fourth pick of the first-round draft. He was only twenty. During his rookie season, Payton was on the field for seven games and rushed for 679 yards. The following year, he rushed 1,390 yards, narrowly missing the NFL rushing title. That year, the Bears' record was 7-7. The following year, the Bears had their first winning season since 1967. Payton led the NFL in rushing with a total of 1,852 yards. Until his retirement from the Bears, Payton played 184 straight games. His career rushing record stands at 16,726 yards, and he delivered one hundred touchdowns.

In 1993, Payton was inducted into the Football Hall of Fame. At the time, Jim Finks said of Payton, "He is a complete football player." During his lifetime, Walter Payton was considered one of the greatest players to ever rush down a football field. His accomplishments demand attention: eight NFL records, including a record-setting 6,726 yards rushing; setting twenty-eight Bears team records during his thirteen seasons with the team; voted to nine Pro Bowl games; elected to the Pro Football Hall of Fame; led the Bears to a 15-1 record season in 1985; and chosen as the Most Valuable Player. In 1977, Payton was presented with the NFL's Man of the Year Award, which was renamed the Walter Payton Man of the Year Award after he died in 1999.

Walter Payton was one of football's most fit players. He honed his body with sheer determination and rigorous training. He ran a steep hill near his home twenty times a day; he could leg press seven hundred pounds and bench press three hundred. Most impressive was his ability to walk across a football field on his hands. Some quietly called Payton "Superman."

After retiring from the Bears in 1987, Payton became involved in auto racing, served on the board of directors for the Bears and ran several businesses the Chicago area. Meanwhile, he took time out to serve as a coach for the Hoffman Estates basketball team that headed for the state playoffs.

Payton's swift and untimely death at forty-five due to a rare liver disease called primary sclerosing cholangitis took everyone by surprise, even his doctors at Mayo Clinic in Rochester, Minnesota, where Walter was being treated. Payton's close teammate and friend Mike Singletary recalls spending the weekend with Walter before his death. The two men read scripture and prayed. Payton's family—wife Connie, son Jarrett and daughter Brittney—were at his side when death came on Monday, November 1, 1999. Coach Ditka called Walter Payton "the greatest Bear of all." He gave us Chicago fans the best time of our lives.

Michael Singletary was born on October 9, 1958, in Houston, Texas. His parents were Charles and Rudell Singletary, and he had several siblings. The family lived in a modest wood-frame home next to the Church of God, which Charles built himself. While Mike was still young, Charles Singletary abandoned his family, leaving Mike fatherless. His brother Grady filled the void and admonished Michael not to drink beer or smoke cigarettes. After attending church services on Sunday, Michael would spend the rest of the day watching the Dallas Cowboys. His favorite players were Roger Staubach, Bob Lilly and Lee Roy Jordan. Michael began playing football when he was in seventh grade. Grady attended his games. Tragedy struck the family when Grady was killed by a drunk driver. Michael Thomas, Singletary's brother-in-law, stepped in and attended the young boy's games. In ninth grade, Michael became an all-state star as a guard and linebacker. Singletary's grades were not strong, but he managed to earn a scholarship to Baylor University in Waco, Texas. While at Baylor, Singletary averaged fifteen tackles per game and earned All-Star honors his junior and senior years. He became a campus legend. He lettered all four years at school and won numerous awards: Southwest Conference, three years; the Davey O'Brien Award as an outstanding southwest conference player; and All-American, two years.

Singletary joined the Bears in 1981 and became a starting linebacker. His football prowess soon shone. In a game against Kansas City, Singletary recorded 10 tackles and 1 fumble. He went on to start 172 games over his twelve-year career with the Bears. He became known as Samurai Mike for his intense gaze into his opponents' eyes and his total focus on the field. In 1985, he listed 109 solo tackles, 52 assists, 3 sacks, 1 interception, 3 fumble recoveries, 1 forced fumble and 10 defended passes. In the New Orleans Super Bowl XX game, Singletary broke up a pass that would have gone for a touchdown, had 2 fumble recoveries and slammed the opposition with his six-foot, 230-pound body. Singletary was named the NFL Player of the Year by the Associated Press in 1985 and 1988.

Singletary went on to coaching positions at his alma mater, Baylor, and with the Baltimore Ravens, San Francisco '49ers and Minnesota Vikings. Michael Singletary now lives in Texas with his wife, Kim, and seven children. Today, the inspirational Singletary is sought by Fortune 500 Companies to be their keynote speaker. He never fails to deliver his message of the need to have a vision, to be the best that you can be.

When the New York Mets drafted Danny Wilson in the twenty-sixth round in 1987, he did the unthinkable: he turned them down, electing instead to attend the University of Minnesota. Wilson rejoined the baseball draft pool in 1990. He was signed by the Cincinnati Reds Organization on September 7, 1992. By the time his rookie year ended, he became one of the league's most skilled catchers. Wilson was born on March 25, 1969, and grew up in Barrington. While attending Barrington High School, he acquired the nickname Dan the Man for his outstanding moral character and outstanding athletic skills. Danny played on the varsity baseball team for four years at BHS from 1984 to 1987. He still holds the school's record for the most pitching wins, shut-outs and strike-outs.

Wilson quarterbacked for the Broncos football team and received All-State honors three times as a hockey goalie and twice as a baseball pitcher and catcher. He led the high school baseball team to a state title with a 13-0 pitching record and a .470 batting average. He also helped his team win the gold medal in the Summer Olympic Festival and was All-Tournament catcher for the United States at the World Junior Games in Canada. Wilson says he learned many life-skills at BHS including "[the need to] have a good work ethic, respect the game, hustle, do your best, strive for excellence and be a team player."

Wilson graduated from Barrington in 1987 and entered the University of Minnesota's (UM) mechanical engineering program. He joined Minnesota's Golden Gophers baseball team his freshman year and garnered high praise. He was a Big Ten Rookie of the Year in 1988. Records show that Wilson gunned down 50 percent of "would be baseball stealers" and seventeen of twenty-one runners in 1990. His offense and defense skills earned him a place in Baseball America. He was an All-American at UM. A major highlight of Wilson's talent happened in 1989 at the Presidential Cup Tourney in Taiwan when he delivered the tenth-inning home run to win the game for Team USA.

DEDICATION   EXCELLENCE   TRADITION

*Above*: Barrington Baseball logo. *Image courtesy of Dave Engle, former BHS art teacher and coach.*

*Left*: Kirby Smith, legendary BHS and American Legion summer baseball coach, anchored many winning seasons. Danny Wilson played for Smith.

The Reds released Wilson after only three years with the franchise. They traded Wilson and Bobby Ayala to the Seattle Mariners in exchange for Erik Hanson and Brett Boone. Lou Piniella, the manager of the Mariners and former manager of the Reds from 1991 to 1992, insisted that Danny be part of the trade because he liked what he saw in the young athlete. Wilson moved to Seattle in 1994, and that year, he represented the Mariners at the All-Star game. During Wilson's decade-long tenure with the club, he endeared himself to his teammates and fans for his consistency as a player, gentlemanly demeanor and community charitable endeavors.

Danny Wilson, BHS class of 1987, has served as a role model for many. Matt Blue, BHS class of 1990, recalls the time when Danny had been drafted by Cincinnati and was looking for a place to work out in the summer before joining his teammates. Danny's former BHS coach, Kirby Smith, invited Wilson to join the American Legion Summer Baseball League. Danny fell right in with the young athletes and participated in their workouts designed to improve endurance, skills and techniques. Patience and humility oversaw all of Wilson's comments to the youthful baseball players. At the end of one practice session, Smith gathered his team on the field to review their day's efforts. While the coach was talking, Wilson took it upon himself to clean all the players' equipment so it would be ready for the next day. When the American Legion team saw what Wilson had done, they realized they had just learned an indelible lesson from a true major league *professional*. Wilson's act of kindness impressed Barrington's young baseball players and reminded them that one should never get too big headed.

Danny Wilson, BHS class of 1987, was dubbed a scholar and a gentleman. He now lives with his wife and four children in Seattle, Washington, and works for the Seahawks.

Wilson enjoyed a nineteen-year major league baseball career. In keeping with his nature, he demurs his baseball skills and considers himself "one of many." Today, Wilson works in the front office for the Mariners. His legion of fans remember him for the man he was as a player, how he played the game and the way he now lives his life. He married his Grove Avenue School sweetheart, Annie Palmer, and the family lives in Seattle with their four teenage children.

Golfer Gary Hallberg's birthday is May 31, 1958. He was born in Berwyn, Illinois, and graduated from Barrington High School in 1976. He turned professional in 1980 after graduating from Wake Forest University. In 1980, Hallberg was chosen Rookie of the Year, his first year as a professional. Hallberg also won PGA tours in 1983, 1987 and 1992.

Hallberg's other championships include the U.S. Open, the Japan Golf Tour and the Nationwide Tour. He has garnered twelve professional wins. Hallberg was the founder of the Pro-Am Saturdays series and headed Hallberg Golf Productions, which ran the Murray Caddyshack Invitational. Hallberg has worked as an analyst for CNBC and NBC sports and now lives with his family in Castle Rock, Colorado.

In 2004, Barrington High School Distinguished Graduate Gary Hallberg returned to the community to assist in raising funds for the District 220 Educational Foundation's golf event. Hallberg took center stage when he gave a golfing demonstration for the attendees and members of the Barrington High School boys' and girls' golf teams at Thunderbird (now Makray Memorial Golf Club). Golfers who failed to clear one of the course's water hazards at one of the holes could pay $20 and opt to have a high-school golf-team member replay the hole. Duffers earned $1,000 for the school's Educational Fund. To lure adult players, three local car dealerships promised a car to any golfers who achieved a hole-in-one; not one of the players went home with a vehicle that day.

Barrington has been a sports center for decades. At the turn of the century, the Barrington baseball team took up residence in Sprunner Park near the Metra train tracks—now the location of the Antique Mall and the Volvo car dealership. The park was named for George Sprunner, who was mayor of Barrington from 1907 to 1909. The park had bleachers on either side of the field and a covered stand behind home plate. Cars parked along nearby Liberty Street, and fans walked across the street to watch the games. At first, the team was known as the Village Team and then, in the 1920s, changed its name to the Barrington Bears. Among the players were men whose names are still familiar in town: Altenburg, Bartholomew, Beem, Berg, Flock, Garish, Homuth, Johnson, Kasch, Schref, Sheehan, Shuett and Wickman. Ward Flock, one of Barrington's most iconic characters, managed the team. Flock had attended the University of Illinois and was a baseball teammate of George Halas. The men were often seen together at Flock's Cow Gate Farm on Route 22. But Flock is mostly remembered as one of Barrington's most colorful men who was often seen driving his wide-winged Cadillac convertible, roof down, in downtown in the middle of winter.

Today, Barringtonians focus on being physically fit while attending many of the athletic venues in the area, including yoga and Pilates studios, fitness centers and bike- and horse-riding trails in or around the village. Center stage for fitness aficionados is the Barrington Park District's Langendorf Park. Its first swimming pool was built in 1931. Today, there are two large pools as well as a wading pool for the community's smallest citizens. Generous tracts of land and several new facilities have been added to the Park by gifts from the Jewel Tea Company, the Lions Club, the Kiwanis Club, the Barrington Women's Club and the DeTomasi and Pepper families. Local citizens approved numerous referendums to raise cash to continue to improve the offerings at the community's parks: Miller, Minehardt, Beese and, the newest, Citizens. Since the Park District opened, there have only been three directors: Richard Miller, Tom Tayler and Teresa (Terry) Jennings. Today, Jennings watches over the sizable Barrington Park District Fitness & Recreation Center, as well as the ever-popular Citizens Park. Her role in the community is vital to its physical and psychic well-being as the Park District offers a plethora of year-round indoor and outdoor activities.

Barrington follows Chicago's sports franchises, but they take most pleasure in their local sports venues, from peewee matches to an array of junior-varsity and varsity high school teams, including football, basketball, baseball, gymnastics, tennis, lacrosse, swimming, diving, wrestling, volleyball, cross country, track and field and hockey—to name some of them.

Coaches play an important role in the lives of the young athletes. Three of BHS's beloved coaches include Tom Frederick, Dave Gehler and Andy Kostick whose years at the high school overlapped and complement one another.

Tom Frederick was born on May 15, 1924. He taught physical education and coached football, baseball and basketball in Waterloo, Wisconsin, before coming to Barrington. He became head football coach at BHS in 1950 when he was only twenty-six. In his first season, Frederick finished 9-0. Tom had a magical way when it came to coaching young athletes. One memorable game came in 1958, when Barrington's homecoming halftime score saw the Crystal Lake team on top with a 25–6 score. In the second half, Frederick's team demonstrated a remarkable rally and beat their opponent 33–25, thanks in large part to the throwing skills of Bill Throp. Under Frederick, Barrington earned six conference titles. When Frederick died of cancer on October 10, 1990, *Daily Herald* assistant managing sports editor Bob Frisk wrote, "Tom spent his years in the high school system thinking of others rather than himself." Frisk goes on, "I hope [the family] know that the impact of Tom Frederick's work in interscholastic athletics is enormous [and] that his legacy will live on forever." There is a stone marker in Tom Frederick's honor south of the entrance to the BHS football field.

Dave Gehler was born on July 8, 1931, in Watertown, Wisconsin, to Harvey and Vivian Gehler. He had a twin sister, Diane, and a younger sister, Mary. He attended the University of Wisconsin–Madison and earned a BS degree in physical education in 1953 and an MA degree in 1957 from the same school. Gehler was recruited by Tom Frederick and took a job as a physical education teacher in 1958. Gehler taught physical education and coached wrestling, baseball and football before becoming chair of the Physical Education Department in 1962. According to reporter Bob Blagemann, "Gehler was head varsity wrestling coach from 1957 through 1963. During that time he compiled a 66-23 dual match record, won one North Suburban Conference championship and coached three state qualifiers: Tom Riggs, Jeff Lewis and Kim Wood." Gehler also announced the Illinois State Wrestling Tournament for ten years, keeping fans enthralled with his smooth and confident voice. In addition, Gehler spearheaded a drive to build a swimming pool at BHS and established the school's Junior/Senior Leadership P.E. Program. Passionate about P.E., Gehler developed a curriculum that became a model for graduate P.E. students at Western Michigan University. Dave loved to fish and spent many weekends on Wisconsin lakes looking for the biggest muskie. To his delight, Dave caught a fifty-three-inch, thirty-

Tom Frederick—popular and, hands-down, one of the most victorious Barrington football coaches—is carried off the field after another triumphant season. *Photo courtesy of Barrington School's Archives.*

five-pound muskie on Lake Namekagon in Bayfield County, Wisconsin. With this fish, he won first place in the annual Hayward Muskie Festival in 1986. He died in Barrington on December 1, 2006.

*Top left*: Win Jones, BHS track coach and Art Department watercolor specialist, later taught art at Northern Illinois University as an associate professor. He moved later Florida.

*Top right*: Coach Andy Kostick specialized in gymnastics but coached freshman football and tennis at BHS for over thirty years. *Portrait by Thomas Balsamo.*

*Bottom*: Art observers call Win Jones's watercolors haunting and ethereal. Jones spent his summers conducting workshops and attending art fairs.

Kostick was hired by Dave Gehler and Tom Frederick after he obtained his MS degree from Southern Illinois University, where he was assistant gymnastic coach to the legendary Bill Meade. Kostick was hired in 1960 to launch a gymnastics program at BHS and was given carte blanche to purchase equipment for the school. In no time, a gymnastics team was formed. Later, Kostick taught the women in the Physical Education Department how to coach and teach gymnastics.

Andy was born on June 19, 1929, in Chicago to Louis (Ukrainian) and Mary (Ukrainian American) Kostick. After graduating from Bowen High School, Kostick enlisted in the army during the Korean War. He was sent to Hanau, Germany. Volunteering to join the U.S. Army swimming and diving team, he earned many first-place trophies and medals at the Berlin Olympic Stadium.

Kostick returned home and began taking classes at the University of Illinois Chicago campus. He took several buses from his home in Hegwich to get to the school. After two years in Chicago, Kostick went downstate to Springfield to complete his bachelor's degree. While at Barrington, Kostick coached gymnastics, tennis and freshman football. He taught P.E. at the school from 1960 until he retired in 1992. Kostick received statewide recognition for his gymnastics prowess when he was inducted into the Gymnastics Hall of Fame in 2008. Many former students, and especially gymnastics team members, attended the ceremony. Recently, one of Andy's former gymnasts, Dave Butzman, made a considerable contribution in Andy's name to the Philadelphia Foundation. Andy is honored at BHS with his name over one of the doorways in the men's gym. To this day, students remember Kostick as a P.E. teacher who joined them in their games, who always had a smile on his face, who embraced non-athletic students in his classes and who radiated a joy of life.

# 5

# Businesses and the People Who Own Them

*If a man has talent and learns somehow to use the whole of it,*
*he has gloriously succeeded.*
*–Thomas Wolfe*

Over the course of Barrington's 150 years, the village has served as its epicenter. Early on, grains were sold out of make-do sheds to farmers for their livestock. In 1854 when the railroad arrived, it altered the way people did business as merchants and their goods flowed into Barrington to be near the train. Nearby residents who lacked shops in their communities came to purchase essential materials. But before the turn of the century, Barrington began to shed its farm-focused shops, and it became a vital retail enterprise.

Today, the village is anchored by two grocery stores, a movie theater, numerous cafés and specialty shops—one-of-a-kind clothing stores for men, women and children, such as Amazing Gracie's Children Shoppe, Grassroots Clothing, Savvy Spirit, Tommy Terri Children's Boutique, Starr Couture and M.J. Miller & Company. There are also many fine food restaurants in the village: Baloney's, Egg Harbor, Chessie's, the Breadbasket, Wool Street Café, Francesca's, Kooker's, McGonigal's Irish Pub, Onion Pub and Eatery, Sagano's Japanese Restaurant, Ciao Baby and the Canteen to name some. It also features jewelry salesrooms and flower shops, as well as banks, both large and small: BMO, Chase and the Barrington Bank and Trust. Barrington is also home to corporate headquarters, research facilities and companies with

Ben Franklin is a prominent feature in this downtown business district photo that also highlights Bert's Tavern and McLeister's Soda Shop. *Photo obtained through the Lake County Museum.*

worldwide recognition, including Pepper Construction Company, Pepsi Co. and, in the recent past, the Jewel Tea Headquarters. Others like Norton's are unique to the community and offer a wide variety of only American-made goods.

For nearly fifty-five years, the smell of freshly roasted coffee at the Jewel corporate campus adjacent to Lake Zurich Road wafted over Barrington. The history of the Jewel Tea Company's move to Barrington is a captivating piece of the community's story.

C.L. Miller, an authority on the company, as well as its famous Autumn Leaf dishware, penned a history of Jewel Tea's development. According to Miller's notes, Frank Vernon Skiff, one of Jewel's founders, was born in Newton, Iowa, in 1869. His family owned a general store where young Skiff learned the trade. The family left Iowa by the late 1800s and moved to Chicago, where Skiff worked for the India Tea Company that sold coffee out of bags, bins and large canisters. While working there, he wondered why freshly ground coffee couldn't be delivered to customers on a regular basis. By 1899, Skiff had $700, a rented horse and a secondhand wagon and began selling coffee door to door in Chicago's Stock Yard neighborhood. In 1902, Skiff partnered with his brother-in-law, Frank Ross. Word spread

Chessie's Caboose stands resplendent in front of the Ice House Mall, where history meets history. On these grounds once stood the Bowman Dairy that served Barrington for decades. *Painting by Mort Luby.*

The Jewel Tea corporate headquarters was built in an Art Deco style in 1929. The building was listed on the National Register of Historic Buildings before it was demolished. *Image courtesy of architect Karl Heitman.*

quickly about the coffee-sellers' amiable manners and their reasonably priced, fresh-ground coffee.

Traditionally coffee sat for months in grocery stores after it was roasted. Homemakers responded eagerly to the freshness of Skiff and Ross's coffee that was delivered on a biweekly schedule. As the core of their clientele grew, so did their customers' desire to have more products delivered to their homes. Soon, the horse-cart service carried fifty food, laundry and toiletry products. At the time, the term "jewel" was synonymous with quality and value. Understanding the importance of branding, Skiff and Ross selected the name Jewel for their burgeoning business. Soon, more routemen were needed to keep pace with the ever-increasing customer demands. Jewel began branching out across the county. In the internal guide for Jewel Company workers, *From Jewel Ways—1916*, it provided its delivery fleet with this advice:

> *Have a piece of cloth in your wagon and a loaf of sugar in your pocket. When you go into the barn (to retrieve your horse), examine your harness and wagon and make sure everything is secure before you leave. Take the cloth and wipe off the imaginary speck of dirt on your horse's nose or neck and feed him the sugar. Talk to him. Say, "Old Jim, we're going after 'em today. We'll make it a big day." Be kind to him. The man who is kind to his horse or mules will be kind to his customers.*

Without their horses, deliverymen knew that they would be out of work and Skiff and Ross would be out of business.

By 1917, Jewel numbered 1,714 routes. But World War I brought the expanding company a set of unexpected problems. Manpower became hard to recruit, costs of raw materials skyrocketed and the government commandeered Jewel's Hoboken, New Jersey coffee roasting plant and turned it into a war-materiel production center. By 1919, Skiff and Ross decided to resign from the company, and Raymond E. Durham and John M. Hancock took the reigns. They began changing the face of Jewel. Routes and branches were reduced to 994. Failing plants were shuttered in New Orleans and San Francisco, but by 1922, the belt tightening measures had paid off. Hancock, a trained veterinarian, resigned from the company and turned his position over to Maurice Karker, who brought with him more innovative ideas.

Of primary importance, in 1933, Jewel introduced an album that shoppers filled with brightly colored stamps illustrating events in Chicago's

Jewel on Main Street is the company's flagship shop in Barrington that opened in 1961. It remains a staple in the community.

history. Next, the company reinstating Ross's idea of advancing the premium, a means by which shoppers could accrue coupons that were packaged inside Jewel products for their albums. Customers redeemed the coupons for premiums that included aprons, blankets and yard goods. Later, the premiums provided homeowners with additional treasures: Club Aluminum, West Bend pots and pans, chrome-plated toasters, floor lamps and shades and the highly cherished bonus—the Autumn Leaf chinaware that became increasingly popular. Today, the chinaware pieces are valuable collectibles.

Karker continued to look for ways to make Jewel's operation more efficient and profitable. He planned to consolidate Jewel's executive offices and its coffee roasting plant to one campus. After an exhaustive study, Jewel Tea Company Inc. hired the internationally famous Chicago architectural firm of Holabird and Root to design its new corporate headquarters. The company planned to create a Jewel Tea Company community where it could expand as a business and find a dependable workforce. Many small cities and villages were considered: Waukegan, Joliet, West Chicago, Elgin and even Kohler, Wisconsin, and Hershey, Pennsylvania. But upon exhaustive examination, it was determined that these locations did not accurately match Karker's vision of a human and environmentally responsible community. Finally, the committee narrowed its search to a "high grade town, purely residential in character, the population of which would not exceed, 5,000." Robert Hilton, assistant to Karker, wrote in *The Story of Jewel's Move to Barrington* reasons Barrington was chosen:

> The village *"approached the ideal for which we sought. If Barrington wanted the company and satisfactory arrangements of all details could be accomplished, Jewel could happily and profitably settle in Barrington."* In addition to its natural beauty and attractiveness, Barrington's proximity to the Elgin, Joliet and Eastern (the E, J&E), the Chicago & North Western railways, and numerous major roadways, fit the Jewel Company transportation needs to a tea. *Hilton continued: "There would be* [in Barrington] *an opportunity for* [Jewel employees] *to live and own an attractive, comfortable home in a most attractive community; living and working in an environment of pure air, sunshine, outdoor life, with time and space for recreation; better physical condition for employees and their families; simple pleasures and lives—leading to savings and independence; opportunities to take part in civic and community life and, finally, sharing the cultural and amusement advantages of proximity to a large city like Chicago without the disadvantages (of) in it."*

The state-of-the-art corporate complex opened in 1930 on the 133 acres of farmland Jewel purchased previously. The lavish Art Deco building featured an abundance of limestone, marble and brass. Later, Jewel added warehouse space and a coffee roasting facility to the site. Then came indoor and outdoor recreation spaces for employees. Karker also arranged for annual summertime fairs and festivals for his workers.

Directed by the legendary landscape architect John Larsons Bell, crews planted fifty-five thousand trees, shrubs and bushes on and around the property. He also planned Jewel Park, where company executives could buy spacious homes nestled beneath stately, sturdy oaks. Jewel Park was located just to the north and west of the company's complex.

After fifty-five years, the Jewel headquarters closed its doors. Just before the building was demolished, a group of hearty souls managed to get the Jewel headquarters added to the National Register of Historic Places. Today, the Barrington History Museum hosts a generous amount of Jewel memorabilia and has plans to create a Jewel store museum on its grounds. Corporate legacy lives on in Jewel's many Chicago stores, including one in downtown Barrington. Its "famous ten marketing principles are held steadfast and include: clean stores with well-organized aisles, consistently friendly service, self-service, honest weights, fair dealings, freshness, quality, good prices [and] money-back guarantees."

Over the course of Barrington's history, it has been home to numerous supermarkets, including National, A&P, Jewel, Eagle and Bockwinkle. Heinen's Fine Foods is Barrington's newest grocery store. Jeff and Tom, co-owners and grandsons of the originator, opened their flagship Illinois store in Shops at Flint Creek on August 22, 2012. Since that date, the duo has opened other stores in the Chicago market. Heinen's features fresh foods, prepared foods and daily baked goods in a spacious, bright and cheery environment. Entering Heinen's is like entering a food art gallery as the colorful displays beckon customers. Employees are friendly and easy to find as they all wear light-blue oxford tops and tan pants.

In 1929, Joe Heinen opened a small butcher shop targeted for residents of northeastern Ohio. Joe always had a vision that his butcher shop could be so much more by adding groceries, dairy and produce, and so in 1933, he moved across the street and opened the first supermarket in northeast Ohio. He built his reputation by selling only the freshest, best food and taught his team to "never sell anything to a customer you would not buy yourself." He excelled in "treating his customers like guests and inviting

Heinen's storefront in the Flint Creek Shopping Center.

them back." He was the quintessential entrepreneur as he innovated year after year. He was the first retailer to sell packaged meat and produce so customers would not have to wait in line at the service counters. He built 330,000 square feet of warehouse to supply his seven stores, unheard of in the industry even today, so he could always control his own destiny as it related to the products he sold and how often his stores received deliveries. He made his own cold cuts, candled his eggs, cut and wrapped his own cheese and made his own salads.

Today, Joe's grandsons carry on the traditions he started by being dedicated to knowing where their food comes from and building relationships with family farmers and ranchers who supply the stores. Heinen's is very committed to local products in its Chicago and Cleveland stores. It believes smaller local food producers demonstrate the same care in making their products as Heinen's does making its own and selling all its products. Tom and Jeff understand, as have all three generations, that the associates making up the Heinen's team are their most important asset, and they are committed to building a family culture and great place to work for all those who join the Heinen's team. The company has always prided itself on being a good community neighbor and tries to support the schools and other events that their loyal customers ask them to support. One of Heinen's goals is to have every customer leave the store feeling better than when they walked in. They achieve this by introducing the customer to great food through demonstrations and also through the associates sharing their vast knowledge of the products they sell. Shopping at Heinen's is an experience much larger than going to buy groceries.

Customers who shopped at Heinen's began asking Joe to offer additional products. By 1933, the shop was selling homemade peanut butter, pickles, donuts, canned goods and fresh produce. Heinen aimed to provide customers with world-class products and first-rate service. Heinen's Fine Foods developed and grew. Today, there are seventeen Heinen's stores in Ohio and four in Illinois. The day-to-day operations are run by Jeff and Tom, who travel outside Ohio to check on their stores. Heinen's provides customers with a chance to taste its cheeses, olives and wines before purchasing these products. Customers can also sample chilies and soups. Heinen's is a full-service store that is gaining a lot of attention in and around Barrington.

Pasquesi's Home and Garden Center is a Barrington destination. The family-owned business focuses on gardening, home and pet supplies. Ed Pasquesi's father immigrated to the United States from Italy. The family traveled from his native land aboard the *Andrea Doria*, the famous Italian ocean liner that sank off Long Island a few months after the Pasquesis arrived in America. Like many immigrants, the Pasquesis settled into a community where their native tongue was spoken, shops carried familiar foods and newspapers were published in their birth language. Gradually, young Ed began to learn English; when he knew enough, he was able to work six days a week at the local A&P in Highland Park. Each of his paychecks was given to his parents. In less than two years, the family saved enough money to buy a car, a TV and a home in Highland Park.

A life-altering event occurred when Ed's father had an appendicitis attack. While his father was recovering at Highland Park Hospital, the elder Pasquesi's nurse, Marie, met Ed on one of his visits to his father's hospital room. They believe that it was love at first sight. The couple married in 1966. At the time, Ed was an apprentice meat cutter at a local butcher shop. By 1970, Ed and Marie had a son, Mike, and a daughter, Cindy; they would later add another daughter, Lisa, to the family. Now they were looking for a family business opportunity. In 1975, they bought a small Ace Hardware store and converted it into Pasquesi's Home and Gardens. Each spring, Marie sold flowers on the sidewalk in front of the store; her clever positioning attracted people inside their shop. When the business expanded and the needs of their customers changed, the store became Pasquesi Home and Farm Suppliers, supporting the many farms in the area. The Barrington location was opened in 1988 when they transformed a car dealership on Route 14 into a home and garden emporium. Then, in 2006, the original store relocated to Lake Bluff, and in 2012, a third, smaller store opened in downtown Lake Forest.

Pasquesi is a home and garden center to be reckoned with. People come from miles away to shop at this pleasant, colorful marketplace. *Photo courtesy of Crystal Pasquesi.*

Pasquesi offers flowers and vegetables for your garden and shrubs for your landscape needs, as well as seasonal decorations for your home. *Photo courtesy of Crystal Pasquesi.*

Today, all three children work at Pasquesi's. Mike joined the team after college and for awhile managed the Barrington store. Now he is the president and general manager of the family enterprise. Of their operation, Mike says, "We are always challenging ourselves and looking for ways to improve our business. We will never stand still. We are constantly learning and trying new and different things." Daughter Cindy serves as the director of human resources, a job that takes advantage of her background in corporate sales and project planning. Of her role, she says, "I mainly focus on recruiting and training employees…Great people help create great experiences, and that will keep the customers coming back." Lisa, the third child, linked up with the family business in 2003. She is now director of marketing for print and web communications. "My main objective is to keep our name and message out there—and we do this through a variety of marketing efforts that show how we think and believe when it comes to our product selections. We strive to create an experience that people want to repeat."

True to the philosophy of Chicago's noted retailer Marshall Field, who declared, "Give the lady what she wants," the Pasquesi family has a respectable reputation for providing attentive customer service and satisfaction. The Pasquesis travel across Europe and other parts of the world to find novel pieces for their home and garden locations. Merchandise comes from Italy, France, Mexico, Greece and Vietnam. The Pasquesis have an eye for what their customers will buy. "We strive to listen to our customers' wants and requests…We are always searching for unique quality home and garden accessories." The stores specialize not only in gifts for the home and garden but also food and treats for birds, dogs and cats. Pasquesi's Home and Garden Center is an oasis of beauty, color and tranquility in an often chaotic world.

Esther Goebbert knew the rigors of being part of a farm family. She swore she would not be a farmer's wife. But when John Goebbert came on the scene, his charming ways led her to marry him, and Esther *did* become a farmer's wife. She grew to relish her role and their seventy-three-acre farm where the family harvested mostly corn and tomatoes, although squash, flowers and pumpkins were also Goebbert's staples.

In 1948, George Goebbert started a roadside vegetable stand in Arlington Heights. By 1972, the family had outgrown their space and bought a forty-acre farm in South Barrington, just north of Higgins Road. Shortly after their move, Jim and his three children began selling pumpkins, and their fall festival became an annual tradition. In 1979, Jim installed the mammoth fiberglass "Happy Jack" pumpkin that sits atop a silo and can be spotted in many directions for quite a distance. Happy Jack measures eighteen feet wide and fifteen feet tall and is an iconic landmark for those seeking a fall adventure. The expansive family pumpkin patch remains one of the largest in Illinois. Schoolchildren and their teachers arrive by busloads, and on weekends, families drive miles to participate in Goebbert's Fall Festival or come in spring to wander among trays of bright-colored annuals and lush blooming flower baskets. Gobbert's is a weekend excursion for many families. In addition to tons of pumpkins, the farm offers hundreds of colorful mums, Indian corn, weathered cornstalks, fruits and vegetables and Halloween decor. There are also freshly baked sugar doughnuts to eat and hot apple cider to sip while visiting Goebbert's. The haunted house is a fall must-do, along with the corn maze and rides on a hay wagon, a pony or a camel. For the past several years, WGN radio's Steve Cochran has broadcasted one of his Halloween-week shows on location at Goebberts. The audience sits atop hay bales, shivering in the pre-dawn barn to watch the live broadcast and sip hot coffee or cider.

Each season offers visitors sights to see and seasonally appropriate merchandise to buy. Today, the Goebbert sons, Lee and Lloyd, along with

Happy Jack atop a silo on the Gobbert Company property. His bright-orange image can be seen from miles around.

their wives and children, continue the family business. The Goebberts celebrated their sixty-fifth farming anniversary in 2013, and their farming tradition rolls on.

Another Barrington landmark is Euro-American Ambrosia Patisserie. When customers enter Ambrosia, located in the Foundry, just north of Northwest Highway, they are sensually transported to a Paris breakfast bistro. Cozy marble tables for two or more line the large plated windows where customers are encouraged to sit and relax, look out on the verdant lawns and pond and put the stress of their lives behind them. Ambrosia's ambiance brims with an appreciation of the good life. This is just the way co-owners Richard and Deborah Rivera like it. They opened their shop in Barrington in 1993 after moving their bakery-bistro from Fox River Grove.

Inside this cherished gathering place, customers are greeted with smells of chocolate, sugar and buttery breads. They see clear-glass display cases that showcase Richard's artistically crafted cakes, cookies and brownies. Standing behind the counter, Debby or one of her meticulously trained assistants greets every customer with a positive attitude, a ready smile and a "How are you today, John?" Debby knows the name of almost everyone who comes into the shop. She is keenly aware that the primary secret to success in the food-service industry is knowing your people. She has worked in or around food since she was fourteen. Her first job was as a bus girl at the former

At Ambrosia, outdoor tables, chairs and bright-striped awnings invite guests to sit and relax, sip a latte and enjoy some delectable sweet and savory items.

Ambrosia's mouth-watering, fruit-laden and chocolate-dipped treats await customers. The smells of the shop make the freshly baked goods irresistible.

Barn of Barrington. In addition, Debby has worked in hotels, restaurants and bars. Her sensitivity to her clients' needs and wishes has earned her, and Ambrosia, a legion of loyal clientele.

Richard and Debby met at the Hyatt Hotel in Schaumburg, where they both were working. Richard's pastry creations merged with Debby's customer-friendly philosophy and created a perfect pairing. Ambrosia has received local and national recognition. It has been featured in *Chicago* magazine, the *Chicago Tribune*, *Ladies' Home Journal* and *Restaurants&Institutions*, as well as in the book *Great Chefs, Great Cities*. On the wall of the shop is a colored photo of Richard and a beaming Julia Child. A signature feature of

Ambrosia's elegant taste is that it tops any boxed goods with an elegant, mini purple and pink orchid that represents Ambrosia's noticeable attention to detail. The shop holds a peerless place in Barrington's business community. It was named "Ambrosia" for good reason.

Norton's USA is a one-of-a-kind, turn-of-the-century-feel general store. It sells items made only in America. Deborah Leydig says her children tease her that her family didn't play store with her *enough* when she was a child. In fact, Leydig set her heart and mind on opening a shop that sold only American-made goods. She wanted to do her part to reverse the trend of goods sold here but manufactured overseas. She put her talents, creativity and vision to work "to dream the unbelievable dream."

Leydig's impressive résumé includes being a fashion designer after graduating from the School of the Art Institute of Chicago, being a graphic artist for fifteen years in the city and being a professional actress. During her role as Barbara Ehrenreich in the stage adaptation of *Nickel and Dimed* at the Steppenwolf Theatre, she noticed a trend that got her to wondering, "Why can't people buy zippers, cording for wrapping paper, or fabrics made in America anymore?" She realized that all these items that were once readily produced in Chicago were now being made overseas. "What can be done to stop this flow?" she wondered.

On June 23, 2007, Leydig opened Norton's USA and set her goal to support American-made goods to work. While driving around Barrington, she noticed that an old livery barn on Lageschulte Street that once housed eight draft horses was for sale. Leydig jumped at the chance to buy the building, and after six months of working with her brother (only using American nails, lumber and other available materials) the team converted the barn into Deborah's vision by creating a unique store where people could shop in a small old-fashioned environment but with a modern experience for a variety of items. Next, she researched places that made products here and began contacting those people. Her first foray into the market yielded 20 companies that could attest that their goods were made in America. Today, her list has grown to over 450 such manufacturers. She finds information about these companies on the Internet, in magazines, at consumer product shows and from suggestions from customers.

Today, Norton's USA sells a vast array of American-made products from pots and pans to purses and ponchos, locally produced jams and honey, area artists' crafted earrings and bracelets, toys, pet supplies, greeting cards, kitchen cupboards, crackers and cookies. Norton's is truly a general store where shoppers can purchase an ice cream cone, a bag of penny

Norton's USA building's façade is colorful and reminiscent of days gone by. Decorations on the building change often with the year-round seasonal celebrations.

Norton's red-white-and-blue items ready you to celebrate the Fourth of July.

candy or a cold bottle of soda or water. Leydig's imaginatively displayed items encourage customers to browse, find a one-of-a-kind present for a family member or friend and in turn allows them to be part of the growing American-made customer groundswell. The store is recognized for its charming ambiance and well-trained, gracious and gregarious staff that is ready to assist shoppers and answer all and any questions. There are so many items for sale that most customers circle the store two or three times to take in all it has to offer.

Deborah says, "Norton's is a store where kids can shop alone and find an affordable gift for mom, dad, a brother or sister, or where they can buy a bag of chips to eat on the way home from school. In addition, it's a place where grandparents can find baby clothes, old-fashioned games, coloring books and more for their grandchildren. We have a lot to offer our varied generational customers."

Deborah works for and donates to community fundraisers. A few projects she supports are volunteering her time to man phone charity lines, setting out colorfully painted Mason jars on her checkout counter to collect coins and bills for the VFW 7706 prior to Memorial Day and hosting an annual cake auction to support Relay for Life. Leydig's store is now woven into the fabric of Barrington. A trip to her shop is like taking a trip back in time and forward into the future. There is something in the shop for everyone.

Dyllis Braithwaite's childhood is one that most of us can only have wished for. She remembers that while she and her siblings slept, her mother was busy sewing new outfits for each of them. "My mother made dresses, suits and other garments to clothe her family," said Braithwaite, who was raised around rich fabrics and a creative parent.

Born in 1927, Dyllis grew up on a dairy farm in rural Winsted, Connecticut. She graduated in 1951 with a bachelor of science degree in

Deborah Leydig sits among Fourth of July celebration flags and banners for sale in her shop.

*Left*: Dyllis Braithewaite, owner of Finn's Fabrics for years, shared her love of creative fashion-making with clients from all over the Northwest suburbs. *Portrait by Thomas Balsamo.*

*Right*: Bill Braithewaite appeared in *Lives with Passion*, sponsored by the Barrington Area Arts Council and the Barrington Area Council on Aging. *Portrait by Thomas Balsamo.*

home economics from the University of Connecticut and taught for three years at Gilbert High School, her alma mater. There she merged her passion for teaching with her love of creating wearable art. Anyone could fashion an apron, but few people could turn out colorful, head-turning, one-of-a-kind ensembles that attracted the attention of onlookers.

With her attorney/husband of sixty-four years, Dyllis moved to the Chicago area and lived on the north shore for several years before moving to Barrington. In 1969, a local shopkeeper, Ellis Finn, hired Dyllis to manage her downtown store—Finn's Fabrics. When Finn retired in 1972, Braithwaite bought the shop, renamed it Finn's Fabrics by Dyllis and doubled the size of the store. She provided rich wools, luxurious silks, soft cottons and every manner of fabric. With her passion for fine fabrics and accessories, Braithwaite traveled the world to discover unique and natural materials with which to fill her shop. Many customers in the Chicago area considered her venue a destination for their tailoring needs. The shop became a center for people to meet neighbors, talk about textiles, see new fashions and cultivate like-minded friendships. Dyllis fostered the special, creative force inside each of her customers, encouraging them to create wearable fashions.

Dyllis started clubs for sewing, knitting and quilting. During the summer months, she offered boys and girls an opportunity to attend her well-regarded Sewing Kamp. Her wish was to spread "the wonder of wearing something you designed and sewed" throughout the community and beyond.

Her loyal customers agreed that seeing an outfit that Dyllis created encouraged them to do likewise whenever they came into the shop to purchase some of its hallmark products: colorful, textured and vibrant pieces of cloth. At each opportunity, Dyllis assured customers that, with due diligence, they too could stitch together a garment similar to hers.

Braithwaite had to close her store after nearly four decades due to health reasons. Since that time, she has been working on her books *Oh! I Love What You're Wearing*, volumes I and II. These colorful, page-turning books feature photographs of Dyllis's enlivened, gorgeous personal collections of wearable art. To this day, total strangers stop Dyllis to comment on her self-created "collage outfits" that are often enhanced by a complementary large broach, hat, scarf or shoes. She is a walking artist's palette. This "material girl" misses the people she served and the spirit of artistry they shared through Finn's Fabrics, but she knows she has had a long and rich life. Dyllis and her husband have three grown children and five grandchildren. She is often seen at the Barrington summer farmers' market, where she is always fashionably dressed from head to toe.

When Floyd Lawrence Bateman was a young teen in Nebraska, he went to work for a railroad company to help his mother, Josephine Boyce, after his father, Selim James, deserted the family for reasons still unknown. Enchanted by trains and a lust for wandering, Bateman rode the rails through most of the states. In 1897, he moved to Chicago and took college night courses. At the turn of the century, Floyd married Alta Aspinwall, a registered nurse from Kearney, Nebraska. They settled into their home on Lake Street in Wilmette. Three children were born to the couple: Floyd Donald, Lawrence Ford and Barbara Jean (Corbett). The growing family later resided on Michigan Avenue in Wilmette.

Floyd Bateman rose in the business ranks, and in 1928, the family moved to a farm in Barrington Hills, where he had herds of horses and prize-winning Black Angus. One evening while the family was sitting on their terrace having cocktails, they witnessed smoke billowing from one of the barns on Horseshoe Road (now Bateman Circle). They raced to see what was going on but realized that they were too late to rescue their treasured horses and blue-ribbon Black

Angus. Fires were commonplace in those days when old barns were struck by lightning and firefighters were miles away. Circa the late 1950s, yet another lightning bolt destroyed the main barn across from the current Barrington Riding Center.

"The whole barn was enveloped in fire with large flames reaching a long way up in the sky," recalls Michael Bateman, one of Floyd and Alta's nine grandchildren. "Really quite spectacular with the fire reflecting off the low rain clouds." No animals were lost in the second fire, but "tractors and other equipment became melted blobs."

The Batemans transformed the original house into a country estate with elaborate architecture and lavish gardens attended to by Alta. In the custom of the

A Bateman family photo of the children: Floyd Donald, Barbara Jean and Lawrence Ford. Their mother, Alta Aspinwall, sits with her children. *Photo courtesy of Peter Bateman.*

day, the road leading to the principal property was named after its owner. Daughter-in-law Charlotte once said, when asked if her family might be related to Bateman Road, "No, Bateman Road is related to us."

Floyd Lawrence Bateman's 1921 passport described him as five-nine, having a high forehead, brown eyes, fair complexion and round mouth. It is easy to picture this gentleman in a dapper three-piece suit, with a fiftieth-anniversary Gruen pocket watch tucked inside his vest, carefully affixed to a gold chain.

Bateman was president of Rotary of Chicago, the first club of Rotary International, from 1929 to 1930 and during his tenure was well regarded by its members. Today, Rotary International boasts of 34,282 clubs with approximately 1.2 million members. When Bateman was hospitalized in 1930, the switchboard at Evanston Hospital was flooded with over three hundred calls from Rotary friends and concerned citizens inquiring about his condition. People who knew or worked with Bateman considered him an exceptionally moral man and a model for others.

*Left*: Copy of Bateman's International Exhibition ticket. *Photo courtesy of Peter Bateman.*

*Right*: Floyd Lawrence Bateman poses for an official portrait. His dignified demeanor bespeaks of his important position among Chicago businessmen and Barrington's countryside gentry. *Photo courtesy of Peter Bateman.*

Floyd Bateman and other businessmen conceived the idea of another Chicago World's Fair that they hoped would open in May 1933. With its emphasis on technological advancements and new inventions, the fair was dubbed the "Century of Progress" but became known as "Rainbow City" due to its colorful buildings and exhibits that stood in sharp contrast to the 1893 fair known as the "White City." In the midst of the Great Depression, the fair was a beacon of hope to millions of people. So successful was the fair that it was extended a year beyond its original closing date.

Bateman became president of the Trans-Continental Freight Company in Chicago when he was thirty. While working in the city, he took an active role in several municipal and national organizations, but the Bateman family still held special allegiance to their hometown. They were committed to Barrington. Floyd served as president of the Barrington Hills Country Club, was the first president of the Countryside School Board and became director of the First National Bank of Barrington.

Floyd Bateman impacted the city's rich and famous as well as Barrington's steadfast and ordinary citizens. While his grandson Michael was living in the village on Summit Street, an elderly former CNW railroad conductor who lived nearby asked Michael if he were related to Mr. Floyd Bateman. Michael replied, "Yes." The conductor commented that Mr. Bateman was a wonderful gentleman who always took time to talk with him and the other train conductors. The man's sincerity was apparent, and he seemed a bit emotional remembering Michael's "Bompy."

Floyd and Alta Bateman remained on their estate until their deaths in 1949. Few men rise from the bottom of the ladder to outstanding success—fewer achieve these heights and retain the admiration of all whom their lives have touched. That perhaps is the best tribute to a Nebraska farm boy who set out to fulfill the American dream and did.

In 1942, Philip E. Bash joined the navy and served as the captain of a submarine chaser in the South Pacific. After the war, he joined the firm of the Leo Barnett Advertising Agency, where he was an advertising executive. Later, he was president of the Clinton E. Frank Advertising Agency. Meanwhile, he spent six years as board chairman at the Garrett Theological Seminary. He said, "These were the best years of my life." Later, he decided to strike out on his own. He and his wife, Flo, married in March 1944, settled in Barrington and raised four children in the community. During the 1970s and 1980s, he left his imprint on the Barrington Historical Society. As director of the historical society and because of Bash's passion for the community and his gift of persuasion, the historical society acquired its property on Main Street and its two historic buildings: the Kincaid and Applebee houses. Bash published the *Barrington Courier Review*.

Bash oversaw the publication of the 1976 Barrington Bicentennial Commission sponsored book *Tales of Old Barrington* by Cynthia Sharp "whose purpose was not to create a history book...but to become a group of tales about life in the prairie village of Barrington...from 1834...until 1920."

Bash died on December 1, 2005. His impact on the community is still deeply felt. During funeral services for Bash at the United Methodist Church, speakers recalled his "love of life, love for people, love of God, love of

Phil Bash, our man about town. *Photo courtesy of Thomas Balsamo.*

The Dockery family's Gold Star Moving business began on February 15, 1918. Pictured is a Model T chain-driven truck. *Photo courtesy of Bruce Dockery.*

learning and love for his community." Barbara, his eldest child, said of her dad, "He was always game for the next journey." Daughter Amy remembered her dad as "an off-the-chart" extrovert. His granddaughter Chloe said she would cherish his pocket offerings, filled with "poems, prayers and testaments to his appreciation for life." Bash's spirit radiated in every realm he entered, in every organization he was part of and in his wide-flung admiration society of family and friends. Phil Bash was a quintessential Barrington figure.

Bruce Dockery's family arrived in Barrington following the pattern of many immigrant families. His grandfather came to America from Germany via Ellis Island and found work and lived in New York for several years. With land available in the West, he took his family down the Erie Canal by boat and overland to Illinois, settling in Chicago. When the city grew too crowded, the family moved again, this time northwest of the city to Barrington, where the Dockerys bought land and began farming. Winters were brutally cold and snowy, and the summers were dangerously hot and humid. But America was a land of promise to anyone who worked hard and honorably.

Tom Dockery started Gold Star Motor Service in Barrington in 1918. The company served Chicago and the northwest suburbs for generations, moving freight between midwestern cities. Thomas's son Ronald L. Dockery was born on August 31, 1936, in Elgin. Ron graduated from Barrington High School in

1954 and attended Wesleyan University. Ron and his brother, Bruce, took over Gold Star Motors, which became ADCO Van and Storage in 1956. Ron was a member and past president of the Barrington Rotary (noon) Club; he had perfect attendance from when he joined in 1974. Ron was one of the founders of the Buffalo Grove Rotary Club. He was very active at the local and district levels, Rotary Youth Leadership Awards chairman for several years, active in the Interact Club at Barrington High School and served as awards chairman for the Rotary District. Ron was a member of the Barrington Area Chamber of Commerce and the Barrington Masonic Lounsbury Lodge #522, as well as the Carpentersville Royal Order of the Moose. He served as a volunteer for Hospice of Northeastern Illinois (now Journey Care) and also enjoyed golf, bowling, fishing, dancing and traveling.

## Do You Remember These Former Barrington Businesses?

*I cannot but remember such things…that were most precious to me.*
*—Shakespeare's* Macbeth

Today, the town boasts of long-serving, generational shops like B. Chones, Hometown Barber, Baloney's, Kranz and Hollis Brothers, to mention a few. But many local businesses that served Barrington for decades no longer grace the community—businesses like McLeister's Soda Shop, which was located on Park Street and featured homemade candies, milkshakes and banana splits. McLeister's drew after-school crowds and Saturday morning shoppers

Warren Sunderladge has operated the Hometown Barber Shop near the Metra tracks on Main Street since 1996. Warren has worked in the shop since 1973.

Davenport Family Funeral Home is among the oldest businesses in Barrington. It began operations in 1865.

who sat on round, aluminum, red-seated stools at the shop's soda bar and discussed the day's events. The list below represents bygone businesses. Remember them and where they were located?

| | |
|---|---|
| Aeroquip Corporation | Barrington Review |
| ADCO Van and Storage | Barrington Bistro |
| American Can Company | Barrington Bootery |
| Anderson's—Ben Franklin | Barrington Camera Shop |
| Anderson's Oil Company | Barton Stationers |
| Annie's Bakery | Baskin Robbins 31 Flavors |
| Archer's Bootery, Inc. | Bells' Apple Orchard |
| Barn of Barrington | Bender-Riger - Pontiac |
| Barrington Classic Cleaners | Bert's Bank Tavern |
| Barrington (Union) Hotel | Bierkness, Ed.—Chevrolet |
| Barrington Chrysler-Plymouth | Bob and Betty's |
| Barrington Paint and Glass | Bob's Sinclair Service |
| Barrington Realty—H. Walbaum | Bockwinkle Grocery Store |

Bowman Dairy (now Ice House)
Bravos, Lou—Oldsmobile
Bob Burros Chevrolet, Inc.
Charlotte's Pizza
Chicago Aerial Industries
Conrad's Variety
Corner Cupboard
Country Butcher Shoppe
Country Cousin Clothing Shop
Creet Blacksmith Shop—Tom
Cuba Electric Shop
Dairy Queen
Darkens Sporting Goods
Deli Dog (Italian Beef)
Drover's Barrington—Chrysler
Eagle Grocery Store
Esh Pharmacy
Fabbri Coiffure
Finn's Fabric
First Federal Savings and Loan
Flying Feather Pet Shop
Freund Brothers, Inc.
Geiske's Steam Laundry
Gold Star Moving Company
Graham Radio & Television Service
Grebe Hardware
Green Grille—Abe Greengard
Hal-Mel Motors—Ford
Hager Lumber
Mrs. Hanie's Bakery
Hank's Standard Service Station
Harv's Barber Shop
Chuck Hines
Honquest Fine Furnishing
Hutchings Barber Shop
Ideal Delicatessen
Jacobson Drugs
Jefferson Ice House
JFK Health World

Johnson Bookseller
Knitter's Nook
Lageschulte Electric
Lageschulte Lumber
Lamey Building
Landwer, Garret—Storekeeper
Langdon's Portrait Photography
LaSalle Bank
Lawn & Garden Shop
Les Tissue Corbet
Lipofsky's Department Store
Lou's Men's & Boy's Shop
Marie's Bakery
McLeister's Soda Shop
McIntosh, M.B.—Lumber Yard
  and Realtor
Meyer's General Store
Morrice & Heyse Motor, Inc.
  (Rambler Auto)
Nancy's Women's Clothing
National Foods Grocery
Nelson Realtor
Northwoods Lumber (Lageschulte)
Noyes Animal Hospital
Old Heidelberg Inn—Barrington
  Hills
Paulson's Lumber Yard
Pedersons '66' Service
Plagge's Hardware
Pohlman's Pharmacy
Pomery and Wesolowski—Flour
  Mill
Quaker Oats Company
Ray's Barber Shop
Reggie's Tavern
Sabin's Saloon
Sandman's Grain Elevator
Satin Filly
Saturday Morning

Shrinner's Meat Market
Schroeder's Hardware
Schroeder's Ford
Schauble Brothers & Collins—
    Buick/Pontiac
Shell Gas Station
Shurtleff's Lumber & Building
    Materials
Standard Oil Station
Stark Realty
Sterlen-Pieper Funeral Parlor
Stott's Grocery Store
Tastee-Frez
Time Shop Jeweler
Tomandl Interiors
Ten-Pin Bowl
Townee Shop
The Toy Shop
Queen's Ransom
UARCO Inc.
Village Green of Barrington
Yount Ford Sales, Inc.
Wenzel's Fine Jewelry
Wichman Blacksmith Shop

# 6

# *Conservation and Preservation*

> *The most precious things of life are near at hand.*
> *–John Burroughs, naturalist*

American's concern for conservation and preservation was introduced during the presidential tenure of Theodore Roosevelt, a man with enormous vision. During Roosevelt's reign, he oversaw the formation of the U.S. Forest Service and established the Reclamation Act of 1902. In addition, he was responsible for the creation of eighteen national monuments, fifty-one federal bird sanctuaries, four national game preserves and five national parks, and he set aside 150 million acres of national forests for posterity. But the Roosevelt plan to "hand over the water, the woods and the grasses to our children" didn't come to significance in the mind of everyday Americans until the 1960s, when the writings of Henry David Thoreau, Aldo Leopold, Rachel Carson and other environmentalist-naturalists began to seep into and take root in the American conscience.

When the pioneers arrived in the Barrington area around 1830 to farm and settle, they transformed the land to meet their needs. The forests, prairies, marshes and fens were cut and plowed, dredged and diverted. Timber was harvested for building materials, and horse-tall grasses turned into grazing lands while an "eye on profits" further drove these transformations of the environment.

Today, Barringtonians guard their open spaces with the tenacity of fierce gladiators facing predatory animals. Numerous conservation and

The Hill 'n' Dale horse farm scene exemplifies the tranquil nature of much of the Barrington countryside area. *Painting by Mort Luby.*

preservation groups, as well as individual homeowners, keep watchful eyes on any form of overt development in the area. They are jealous stewards of their resources.

As in the past, people are drawn to the Barrington area because of its abundant wildlife, tree-lined streets, open spaces and numerous forest preserves. The Greater Barrington area now boasts of a green network that includes woodlands, savannahs, lakes, wetlands, bogs and forest groves, all sheltering many species of indigenous plants and animals. Protecting this verdant belt requires an array of organizations and eco-friendly centers and an army of citizen-volunteers, all of whom are on a mission to conserve and protect the local habitats. Among the best-known natural venues are Crabtree Nature Center, Baker's Lake and Stillman Nature Center. Organizations like the Barrington Area Conservation Trust and Citizens for Conservation (CFC) also maintain a critical role. In addition, local garden clubs and eco-wise gardeners play their part in keeping Barrington green.

Crabtree Nature Center encompasses more than one thousand acres of rolling, glacier-formed lands under the protection of the Cook County

Forest District (CCFD). Crabtree was purchased in the mid-1960s by the CCFD with the intention of returning it to its pre-settler stage. Over the decades, restoration of indigenous plants and the reintroduction of native animal species have been important tasks at Crabtree. Wild plants are uniquely important to Crabtree because they require less water and are able to thrive on natural fertilizers, as well as supply future nourishment to their surroundings.

Crabtree's website describes its bird environment as "112 acres of woodland, wetland and prairie [that] provides a rest stop along the migratory bird highway. 260 species have been recorded using these habitats, with at least 89 species breeding onsite. Bird watchers can stroll through the trails to view birds along the way or stop at the blind to view the scores of waterfowl in spring and fall."

The preserve is beautiful regardless of the season: "In spring, wildflowers carpet the woodlands. The summer brings blossoms in the meadows and prairies. Fall brings autumnal tones to the forest canopy and the native

May-apples were sometimes called the devil's apple. The plant's leaves spread into an umbrella shape to protect the prominent white flower, which turns into a seed pod.

grasses. Winter brings solitude, broken by the calls of various birds visiting the grounds."

Children and adults visit Crabtree's large exhibition center to learn about and enjoy the indigenous flora and fauna on display and to learn more about the living creatures featured there as well. In addition, there are miles of self-guided trails to coax visitors into exploring the setting that is home to a profusion of wildlife and hardy plants.

The center offers year-round activities including bird and wildflower talks, snowshoe walks, Explore the Forest events and, throughout the year, artist-led art programs. Monthly features include lessons about feathered friends, seasonal colors and prairie plantings. In September, audiences are invited to watch as many as fifty artists paint in the tradition of Monet and other Impressionists *en plein air.* Crabtree Nature Center director Jeff Rapp says, "Art in Nature gives folks a chance to see nature through an artist's eyes. We hope that folks who visit not only enjoy watching the process of capturing the natural worlds through a brush, but may be inspired to give it a whirl themselves."

Crabtree works with other forest preserves in the Cook County system to conduct field research, and it partners with zoos and institutions of higher learning across the country to share the results of its work. According to Chuck Westcott, former Crabtree director:

*Each year the CCFP Resource Management staff issues more than fifty permits that allow researchers to conduct scientific studies on forest preserve land. Data from each project, shared with other forest preserves, allows us to leverage our resources and enrich each other's understanding of the natural world. Researchers throughout the country use CCFP data to inform their work and guide land management, benefiting people, plants and animals.*

Just off Northwest Highway, adjacent to Hillside Avenue, lies Baker's Lake, a natural landscape. However, it hasn't always been a lake; it began life as a peat bog. The bog was formed when the glaciers retreated, leaving behind a deep depression. Because it retained water, the depression filled with foliage and swamp grasses. During Barrington's earliest history, the bog served as a cattle-feeding station for several farming families, including Zebina Edgerton, who owned the land in 1847. He then sold the property to Edward Castle, who, along with his son Lester, raised cattle on the grassy land. In 1854, when the Illinois and Wisconsin Railroad laid tracks, Lester convinced the railroad officials to construct a

The center of attention at Baker's Lake is the rookery, which houses great blue and night herons, egrets, cormorants and countless migrating birds.

tunnel under the tracks so he could move his grazing herd across the road from one feeding ground to another. Lester sold his farm to Spencer Otis Sr., who added a house and a round barn to the property. But sometime in 1925, the bog accidentally caught fire. Some believe that sparks from the railroad set the bog ablaze. In later times, the area was purposely lit on fire to stimulate growth of newer vegetation. Smoke from the burning peat gave off a putrid stench that lingered for days and irritated nearby residents.

In 1984, the island in the center of Baker's Lake was selected as a state nature preserve because it already hosted an enormous bird rookery. In 2000, Commonwealth Edison donated twenty additional utility poles to enlarge the original sanctuary for breeding flocks. An engineer, Robert Sliwinski, was hired to oversee the site. Sliwinski determined the original utility poles were still strong, but several old platforms, created with crossbars and cantilevered arms for bird nests, needed significant repairs. These concerns were addressed when a sum of a half million dollars was donated by several preservation agencies, including Illinois Nature Preserves, Forest Preserve District of Cook County, Will County Forest Preserve District, Landscape Resources Inc., Brookfield Zoo, Wisconsin District of Natural Resources, Commonwealth Edison, Max McGraw Wildlife Foundation and the Village of Barrington.

For years now, interested citizens have collected discarded Christmas trees to be set at Baker's Lake in an effort to encourage egrets, herons, cormorants and the state-endangered Black-Crowned Night Herons to nest at the rookery. Thanks to the diligence of local conservationists, including local scout troops and individuals like Patsy Mortimer of Citizens for Conservation, the Baker's Lake campus is thriving. It is considered Barrington's own natural treasure.

The Alexander Stillman Nature Center is a private, not-for-profit facility focused on environmental education, care of injured birds and land restoration. Paths, bridges and a "bird blind" make it the perfect setting to get up close and personal with nature. The site is nestled on eighty acres of woods, lake and prairie in South Barrington.

The center is named after Alexander Stillman, the donor of the property. Stillman was born on September 29, 1911, in New York City. He graduated from Harvard in 1933. Two years later, he obtained his first passport and began his passion for world travel. During World War II, he served with the U.S. Navy, becoming a lieutenant commander. Stillman's military record

A leggy white egret stands near the western shore of Baker's Lake.

was stellar; he was credited with "the sinking of four enemy Merchant Vessels, two large Fishing Boats and a Whale Killer."

Stillman spent his postwar years on the Penny Road property that he purchased from Harold McCormick of Chicago's International Harvester fame. In 1976, Stillman donated his South Barrington property to the Audubon Society of Chicago, and in 1977, he received a Certificate of Life Membership from the National Audubon Society in recognition of his lifelong support of the natural environment.

Signs along Penny Road in South Barrington invite visitors to Stillman Nature Center.

The wealth of Stillman's sprawling land becomes apparent when walking its trails. Overhead, viewers can spot hawks and owls as well as many nesting and migratory birds. Plant life is also abundant, offering visitors a living education about which plants are native and should be cherished and which ones are invasive and should be eradicated.

Fresh animal tracks indicate the presence of deer, raccoons, opossums, muskrats, mice, coyotes, foxes and other mammals that make their homes in this tranquil wilderness. The center's executive director and newsletter editor, Mark Spreyer, cares for injured birds of prey and provides weekend presentations for the public. A unique feature is that Spreyer offers a rare opportunity for ordinary citizens to photograph the raptors he cares for. Among the birds on exhibit are a screech owl, a great horned owl, a red-shoulder hawk, a peregrine falcon and a turkey vulture. Spreyer uses these raptor programs to develop community awareness by providing pertinent information about these colorful, feathered neighbors. In addition to on-site programs, Spreyer's birds have traveled to schools, civic groups, garden clubs and wildlife conferences over the past twenty-five years. He is legendary for his commitment to teaching others the significance of raptor relationship to the natural ecosystem around us. The Stillman Nature Center is an environment that is distinctively different from others in the area with the authentic feel of a rare ecosystem and a home to treasured and cared-for plants and animals.

An injured barn owl is cared for by the staff at Stillman. Some rehabbed birds can be set free; others cannot. The birds are banded for both research identification and management projects.

Barrington's affair with protecting green spaces goes on unabated. Groups like the Barrington Area Conservation Trust offer conservation advice to homeowners, schoolchildren, garden club members and others dedicated to a greener world.

A profusion of animal species inhabits the peat bogs, marshlands, swamps, lakes and neighborhood yards of Barrington. Wildlife is a staple of the community and includes raccoons, deer, skunks, opossums, foxes, coyotes, turtles, crayfish, snakes and butterflies, to name some. Green spaces abound. In a recent interview in *Quintessential Barrington*, Patsy Mortimer of CFC said, "We just need to protect them—through land acquisition, conservation easements or [on] farmland."

Citizens for Conservation is one of the oldest and most widely recognized conservation groups in Barrington and across the state. Several years ago, the group moved its facility from Ela Road to Highway 22, relocating across from Good Shepherd Hospital. Since 1971, CFC has operated as a nonprofit organization whose goals include: "supporting habitats for birds, butterflies and other pollinators, providing healthier watersheds and offering educational programs to learners of all ages."

CFC relies on the support of local volunteers who range from scouts and school-age children to adults, all of whom share a passion for living spaces and for living things. The organization maintains more than 350 acres of nature preserves in the Barrington area. On September 7, 2013, CFC celebrated its twenty-fifth anniversary as the guardian of the Flint Creek Savannah. To mark the event, CFC provided a variety of earth-friendly activities, including prairie walks, family programs, a folksinger, a storyteller, craft projects and a scavenger hunt.

Flint Creek is largely waving prairie grassland, but an actual, flowing creek winds through the grounds, nurturing the grasses, the wildlife and groves of oak and hickory trees.

CFC offers a host of projects and activities throughout the year. These include sales of native plants and trees, ongoing informational programs, summer nature-study classes, garden tours and restoration of natural environments. Its "green thumb approach" to Barrington's green belt has left a significant imprint on the community.

Barrington attracts ornithologists from far and wide. Its extensive wooded areas invite masses of birds. Some are migrating north or south, nesting in locally provided birdhouses or boxes, trees or barns while other birds reside in the community year-round. Barrington birds are well-fed. Wendy Paulson is a woman whose mission is to instill an enthusiasm for birds by offering birding lessons to children and adults. She recognizes birds from their songs or calls before she spots them through her binoculars. No stranger to mud on her boots, Paulson has been leading bird walks for more than thirty years.

She is comfortable in the classroom; Paulson started her career by teaching in Boston public schools. In the 1970s, after moving to Barrington, Paulson was hired to rekindle the once-flourishing Nature Lady Program, funded by the Garden Club and Little Garden Clubs of Barrington, for School District 220 and St. Anne's School. She also developed the

Sam Oliver, director of CFC, sits at her desk monitoring the growth of the organization that promotes bird walks, as well as overseeing the health of nearby creeks, fens and preserves.

Wendy Paulson leads a group of early Saturday morning birders on a search for ordinary and not-so-ordinary local and migratory winged creatures. *Photo courtesy of Wendy Paulson.*

educational program for Citizens for Conservation and launched its newsletter, serving as editor for many years.

For fifteen years, Wendy and her husband, Hank, lived in New York City and Washington, D.C. In both cities, Paulson taught classes about birds in the public schools. Later, back in Illinois, she helped create Openlands' Birds in My Neighborhood program for the Chicago public schools. In addition to her birding work, she serves or has served in leadership positions with many conservation groups, including the Nature Conservancy, Openlands, the Field Museum, Cook County Forest Preserves, Rare and others.

Paulson says, "If your hobby [in her case, birding] is what you love to do, it can be central to what you do for a living." She and her husband, Hank, former sectary of the treasury during the George W. Bush administration, also a birder, live in Barrington Hills and have two grown children. They are avid hikers, cyclists and kayakers.

# 7

# Remembering Those Who Served, Those Who Sacrificed

*Wars may be fought with weapons, but they are won by men.*
*—George Patton*

Like young people in small towns across America, Barringtonians have lined up to serve their country when called. Military records show that they have volunteered since the War of 1812, when eleven men from Barrington fought the British and Indians in their war with America. Colonel George Waterman, a veteran of that war, arrived here in 1842. His family took up farmland in the area along Penny Road. The family farmhouse is recognized in photos in numerous histories of Barrington. Other men were not as fortunate as Waterman, and three of them became causalities of the war and are buried in Miller's Grove Cemetery.

When President Lincoln declared Civil War in 1861, 179 men from Barrington enlisted. They served in cavalry and infantry units from Kentucky to Georgia and Missouri to Tennessee. Some died on the battlefields, many died of unsanitary camp conditions and others died due to lack of sufficient medical aid. War records at the Barrington Township Office list the names of Barrington pioneers who paid the ultimate price among them: Applebee, Hawley, Hiram, Miller, Otis, Wilmarth, Flecher, Freeman, Pierce and others.

Many people believed the Civil War would be brief and the men would be back home in a few months. Little did they imagine that the bloody battles would last for four years and take more of the country's citizens than any previous war. Community groups assisted in the war effort by making and sending provisions to the recruits in battle camps, hospitals or Rebel prisons.

The "boys in blue," as the Northern troops were called, came home no longer boys, but war-scarred men. The human cost of the war was staggering: 350,000 Union soldiers died, including one battle that took 130,000 lives. The number of wounded men, many amputees, was said to be over 280,000. Saving the Union and ending slavery came at a great cost. There are no unwounded soldiers. No one returns from war unchanged.

Some returning soldiers openly talked of their experiences while others remained forever silent. To them, the war was over and they were done with it. These men knew that when they discussed the war, they were carried back to the battlefields, back to carnage, back to the nightmare of war. Liberation to end the fighting came slowly; forgetting the horrors of war took even longer. Often the topic of the conflict among veterans was dropped as quickly as it was raised.

After the Civil War, the Grand Army of the Republic (GAR) was organized as a nonpartisan association composed of honorably discharged soldiers. Its purpose was to assist needy survivors, foster memorials and preserve battlegrounds. Some of these groups formed posts. In 1882, Barrington's post was assigned #275. The post and interested citizens worked together to erect a Civil War statue. On September 6, 1906, spearheaded by the Women's Relief Corps #95, the sculpture was unveiled at Evergreen Cemetery, where it still stands tall guarding souls in village cemetery. A large stars-and-stripes flag flies high on a pole where it is visible 24/7.

By all accounts, World War I, or the Great War, as it was originally called, was an unnecessary conflict. Had prudence or common sense

This VFW logo stands amid the plaques at the War Memorial plaza in downtown Barrington.

prevailed, the clash of arms could have been avoided. Unfortunately, wisdom did not prevail. Diplomats worked to avoid war, but armies *planned* for war. President Wilson and Americans avoided involvement in the European conflict as long as they could, but German U-boats continued to attack U.S. oceangoing merchant ships. When they torpedoed the *Lusitania*, sinking it, Wilson went before Congress on April 2, 1917, to ask for a declaration of war. After Congress declared war, the military set up a draft board in Barrington, housing it in the Blocks

Building on South Cook Street. A new generation of young men volunteered to serve their country once again.

Rationing followed hard on the heels of war. It became a staple of American life. Posters encouraged all Americans to do their part for the war effort: "Every Garden a Munitions Plant," asking citizens, "Will you have a part in Victory?" and reminding them to "Write to the National War Garden Commission—Washington, D.C. for free books on gardening, canning & drying." Other posters declared, "Victory is a Question of Stamina." Each family received ration books that included different colored stamps to obtain different kinds of groceries. Among items limited for purchase were butter, cheese, wheat, meat, sugar, gas, scrap metal, tires and other materials deemed needed

A typical uniformed American doughboy ready to be shipped overseas. *Author's collection.*

for the war effort. Shoppers earned points for every pound of animal fat they collected in cans and turned in to a shopkeeper. These fats were used in making paint and munitions. Everything was needed to help a country at war. American soldiers and civilians experienced hardships throughout the European campaign. The conflict cost three monarchs their thrones: the German kaiser, the Austrian emperor and the Russian tsar. Hopeful again, Americans believed that the war would be brief and that the troops would be home by Christmas—wishful thinking.

With America's inclusion in the European war, its music industry churned out songs for draftees to learn to sing as a means of creating a sense of we're-in-this-together spirit. Soldiers sang "The Caissons Go Rolling Along," "Anchors Aweigh," the "Marine Hymn" and, most often, the wildly popular George M. Cohan "Over There." The war required financial support as well as materials and men; to help pay for the war, the government issued liberty bonds, which were highly promoted

World War II vets Harold Lipofsky (front, center) and Ray Tourville (back, left) march to Evergreen Cemetery for the annual Memorial Day Parade.

Burnell Wollar (right) still fits in his World War II uniform. He and a fellow vet attend a BMS annual Prairie Campus breakfast honoring local vets. Eighth-grade students hear a presentation by their classmates and vets about the importance of safeguarding our freedom.

by celebrities like Al Jolson, Mary Pickford, Douglas Fairbanks and Charlie Chaplin.

After the war ended, each year on November 11, or Armistice Day, America began honoring the men and women who had served. Today it's known as Veterans Day. Celebrations included flag waving, graveside services, gun salutes and other celebratory ceremonies. Barrington's doughboys came home—many with war wounds. Nine of them were killed in action and are buried at the Evergreen, White or St. Paul's Cemeteries.

Unfortunately the "war to end all wars" planted the seeds for World War II. The harsh terms of the Treaty of Versailles, which ended the conflict, fostered years of bitterness throughout Europe but especially in Germany. Economic, social, political and diplomatic wounds festered under the surface and guaranteed that soon the next generation would make even worse geopolitical mistakes that would lead to an even bloodier global war.

Americans declared neutrality when the Axis powers attacked the Allies, but when America found itself thrust into the conflict with the early-morning attack on Pearl Harbor on December 7, 1941, America responded. The next day, President Franklin D. Roosevelt went before Congress to seek a war authorization. Barrington rallied around FDR and sent 648 men and women to serve in Uncle Sam's army. They fought in all corners of the globe and witnessed some of the darkest days of their lives. Eighteen of Barrington's finest died for America's cause. Moved by American soldiers' legendary stories, famed newscaster Tom Brokaw dubbed these warriors the "Greatest Generation." Some of Barrington's greatest who served include Lewis M. Holke, Daniel R. Capulli, Spencer D. Moseley, Henry Sass, Roy G. Etters, Walter G. Moeller, William T. Long, Alfred Munson, Harold Lipofsky, Al Shermer, George Van Hagen, Edmund McGibbon and others. Boy Scout Troop 21 sold bonds for bomber planes under the banner "Buy a Bomber." It was the first Boy Scout troop in the United States to have a "Flying Fortress" named for it. Roy Willmering, whose name appears on the Barrington Scout Cabin today, oversaw the collection of funds sent to the First National Bank or the First Federal Savings and Loan Association.

Two major veterans' organizations were established to assist vets after their terms of service: the Veterans of Foreign Wars (VFW) and the American Legion. Both groups offered war-fatigued soldiers a place to gather, share war remembrances and provide support to one another.

On June 6, 1946, the Barrington Veterans of Foreign Wars Post 7706 was chartered. It had two goals: to assist vets and to help the community. According to post documents, "The VFW Post 7706 served our country

Roy Wilmering Scout Cabin has been home to many scouts for decades. The first boys' troop was organized in Barrington in 1914.

again by supporting the troops and defending our freedom and remembers fallen comrades in funerals and patriotic holidays." On June 13, 2014, President Karen Darch and trustee Jim Daluga hailed the VFW on its sixty-fifth anniversary. World War II veteran and VFW member Burnell Wollar accepted the village proclamation honoring the post. At the podium, Wollar said, "We have dedicated ourselves from day one to their [all veterans'] support and to the village of Barrington." Those in attendance gave the VFW members a standing ovation. The post meets at the Public Safety Building on the second Thursday of the month.

Chartered since 1919, the American Legion's official website lists the organizations' purposes: to uphold and defend the constitution of the United States of America; to maintain law and order; to foster and perpetuate 100 percent Americanism; to preserve the memories and incidents of our associations in the great wars; to inculcate a sense of individual obligation to the community, state and nation; to combat the autocracy of both the classes and the masses; to make right the master of might; to promote peace and goodwill on earth; to safeguard and transmit to posterity the principles of justice, freedom and democracy; to consecrate and sanctify our comradeship by our devotion to mutual helpfulness. Barrington's American Legion Post 158 was organized in 1919 with 89 members. By 1952, it had swelled to 210 members. Today, it boasts 140 members who meet the third Thursday of each month at the Village Hall.

Three of Barrington's men who served during World War II and are living in the community today include John Papamarcos, Vernon Heeren and George Van Hagen. Papamarcos enlisted in the merchant marine from his home in Brooklyn, New York, in 1943. "This was the best decision of my life, and it decided my whole life," said John.

Because he had an engineering degree (BEE), John was accepted into a special United States Maritime Service training facility at Hoffman Island in New York Bay. It was called Prospective Licensed Officer Program (PLO). Papamarcos served aboard T2 tankers that had a turbo electric drive that delivered much-needed gasoline, deck loads of fighter planes and fuel for the navy. After six months' sea time, license exams could be taken to raise the license grade in steps from third assistant to chief engineer. John quickly moved up, becoming a chief engineer in October 1946. John served on ships that delivered supplies across the globe from Liverpool to Belfast, Naples, Guadalcanal, Honolulu, Guam, Singapore and Suez. He was honorably discharged from the United States Coast Guard (which oversaw the merchant marine) on August 15, 1945. He continued to accept assignments to different ships, working for the same company until 1948 supplying cargo around the world wherever it was needed.

After leaving the merchant marine, John and others in this service received no benefits—no GI Bill tuition for education, no Veterans Affairs medical care, no pension, nothing. In 1988, the government deemed it appropriate to allow these veteran seamen to qualify for veteran status. Mainly this allowed them to qualify for benefits at VA hospitals across the country. Of course, many of these veteran seamen were no longer alive.

After the war, John Papamarcos "received a thank-you letter from President Truman written to merchant marine service members. Included with the letter was a Victory Medal attached to a ribbon with thin stripes of red, white, blue, green and yellow. The medal has the merchant marine emblem on one side and the inscription "World War II" on the other. After several jobs, including college instructor and two overseas jobs, Papamarcos took a job in Barrington working for the Technical Publishing Company as an editor of an engineering magazine for the next twenty-six years. He and his wife, Barbara, raised four children in the community: John, Andy, Paula and Mark.

*Left*: John Papamarcos, merchant marine, traveled the world's seas during World War II aboard ships carrying supplies to our men in uniform. *Photo courtesy of John Papamarcos.*

*Below*: A letter received by John Papamarcos after serving in World War II. *Photo courtesy of John Papamarcos.*

*To you who answered the call of your country and served in its Merchant Marine to bring about the total defeat of the enemy, I extend the heartfelt thanks of the Nation. You undertook a most severe task- one which called for courage and fortitude. Because you demonstrated the resourcefulness and calm judgment necessary to carry out that task, we now look to you for leadership and example in further serving our country in peace.*

Harry Truman        February 11, 1948        The White House

Vernon Heeren was nineteen when he volunteered for duty with the army air force. He graduated from flying school at Altus, Oklahoma, in March 1944 and was commissioned a second lieutenant. In June, he and others left Newport News, Virginia, by boat for an undisclosed destination that later turned out to be Naples, Italy. Ten days later, he was assigned to the 441st Squadron and began training to fly B-26s for combat duty.

The United States Army Air Force flew the speedy bomber Martin B-26 Marauder from bases at Midway, the Aleutians, Guadalcanal, Australia, New Guinea, North Africa, the Mediterranean, France, England, Holland, Belgium and here in the United States. Many of these planes went on to complete over one hundred missions. Heeren first flew as co-pilot and then became pilot in a squadron of twenty-seven aircraft. His first missions were in northeast Italy near Lake Como. It was in this arena that Heeren's fellow pilots encountered German ME-109 fighter planes. "On one mission, they made a head-on pass and knocked down six or seven aircraft. They also damaged several others. Only half the planes came back in formation; others limped back on their own," Heeren recalls.

Vern Heeren joined the army air corps right out of high school. After serving missions in Italy and other locales, he spent time serving the U.S. war effort in France.

During George Van Hagen's freshman year at Cornell, Japan attacked Pearl Harbor. Van Hagen joined the navy air corps. In 1945, his F6F "Hellcat" fighter was shot down in the Pacific Ocean near mainland Japan. He survived when "a seaman from an escorting destroyer dove overboard and pulled him unconscious from the sinking plane." At an annual Veterans Day Breakfast at Prairie Middle School honoring vets, one student asked Van Hagen, "Were you afraid?" "Of course," he answered. "But prayer and preparation saw me through." Many who survived the war echoed Van Hagen's remarks. World War II proved to be the most destructive conflict in human history. It was apparent that the Allied forces could not have won the war without America's men, women and munitions.

In honor of the rich history of America, Van Hagen wrote the following:

*The American Homestead*

*I am the cornerstone of America. My heritage is the block-house of John Smith, the plantation of Washington and Jefferson and the log cabin of Lincoln and Jackson. I was born in the early wilderness of this Nation. I have known the trials of independence and heard the stirring words of the patriot. I watched as we were torn by civil war and rejoiced as peace and reason came once again into our Land. I traveled West with the covered wagon and understood the challenge of the frontier. I have known all people and endured all things. I have seen great cities grow in the tide of your industry and felt the productive strength of free men. I have lived to shelter you against the storm and cold and stood with patient devotion in your hours of triumph or need, asking only that I might serve. I have nourished the ideals of freedom and fired your children with the wisdom to build and courage to dare, that is America. I have stood with my face toward heaven, as the bulwark of a great democracy and I will stand evermore if you will help to keep me strong. I am the cradle of hope and dignity. I am the roots of this Land.*

I am the American Homestead.

*(Copyright, 1976).*

Laura Hillenbrand's recently published can't-stop-reading-it biography and movie called *Unbroken* is the story of Lieutenant Louis Zamperini's

George Van Hagen, World War II vet, salutes fellow vets on the occasion of a Memorial Day breakfast gathering. *Portrait courtesy of Thomas Balsamo.*

*Left*: Paul Corwin, Vietnam vet and member of VFW Post 7706, speaks to a crowd at Evergreen Cemetery on Memorial Day 2015 that also celebrated Barrington's Sesquicentennial.

*Below*: Vets march in a post–World War II Independence Day parade down Main Street. *Photo courtesy of Barbara Lipofsky Marsh.*

account of his life as a POW in the Pacific theater. The richly worded biography helps enable us to understand and appreciate the enormous sacrifice American soldiers have endured to save our nation and our world.

Barrington continued to send its "best and bravest" to battlefields in Korea, Vietnam, Kuwait, Iraq, Desert Storm, Afghanistan and Iraq. We honor these men and women with parades on Memorial Day and the Fourth of July. Many of these vets meet with area students and scouts throughout the year to provide lessons on flag etiquette and military history as well as to recount their war experiences. American Legion Post 158 also grants a $4,000 scholarship to a Barrington High School senior and pays for four high school juniors to attend a weeklong summer program at Eastern Illinois University where they study U.S. government. The legion also supports a Barrington summer baseball league program that has been national champs.

The history of Barrington's part in combat is voluminous. The community has been active in its patriotic duty to the nation when summoned. Patriotism and our American traditions help bring us together even when the nation seems divided. We must remember our vets and their sacrifices as we enjoy peace, freedom and prosperity. We must preserve their stories.

On May 28, 1918, President Woodrow Wilson approved a suggestion by the Women's Committee of the Council of National Defenses that women wear a black band on their upper left arm with a gold star affixed for each member of the family who died in defense of the United States. This tradition began in World War I when white service flags with red borders and a blue star in the center for each active member of the U.S. military were displayed by businesses, schools, churches and families in support of our troops. The lists on the following pages show the members of Barrington's history who served and are buried in local cemeteries.

## THE WAR OF 1812

Cyrus Haven

John Hendrickson

Timothy James

Francis H. Kelsey

Lewis Light

Reuben Stevens

John Seymour

George T. Waterman

## CIVIL WAR (1861–65)

Nathan B. Abbott

David Briggs

Arod Cady

Benjamine F. Cockerton

Hiram D. Corbin

Anson C. Davis

William H. Davis

Ira C. Delano

Alphonzo E. J. Devol

Vangordon Dudley

Horce R. D. Freeman

Thomas Gothard

Hiram Hawley

Henry Jackson

Christian Jedder

Gustav Krahn

Justius B. Lane

Charles Long

George W. Miller

John O'Connell

Williams H. Rollins

Merrill H. Sabin

Garret W. Searls

Gilbert Sjerwood

James W. Smith

Albert Stetson

Silas Sutherland

August Topp

Alexander T, Weaveer

Ausust Wilburb

## SPANISH-AMERICAN WAR (1898)

Frederick Lindeers

## WORLD WAR I (1918–19)

Frederick G. Ahlgren

Merill Boyer

Clarence E. Catlow

Jesse L. King

Stanley Marion

Thomas McGraw

Joseph W. Nelson

Otto Radke

Leo L. Sandman

## WORLD WAR II (1941–45)

Raymond Adams

Ernest Anderson

Warren Ankele

George Benson Jr.

Raymond Bidwell

Laddie Dolicek

Robert Gaulke

William Gross

Lyle Hick

George Landwer Jr.

Bruce McGaughy

Robert McLaughlin

Edward Mitchell

Harold Plagge

Jack Roth

Gordon Schlottman

Raymond White

William Webbe III

## KOREAN WAR (1950–53)

Robert K. Kampert

Robert K. Kensel

John F. Popp Jr.

Spencer R. Watt

## VIETNAM (1964–73)

Walter R. Grove Jr.

Edward T. O'Brien

Information provided by Paul Corwin, VFW Post 7706

8

# *Volunteers and Philanthropists*

A *Volunteer's Ode*

*What I have spent is gone.*
*What I have kept is lost*
*What I have gained in doing*
*for others—*
*Will be mine forever.*
*—Anoymous*

No nation has a better track record than America when it comes to donating time and money. In 2011, Americans donated $298 billion to countless causes. They have also donated time for volunteering at schools, hospitals, senior centers, churches, soup kitchens, animal shelters and other worthy causes. Why are Americans so generous? Because they have learned that reaching out to assist others is the surest way to make a difference in someone's life and that a byproduct of giving is that it makes the giver's spirit soar. Giving creates a community sense of interconnectedness. Some local, national and international organizations have giving as part of their bylaws, part of their creed. Psychologists tell us that the happiest people are those who help others.

Barrington has a legacy of civic service. There are over three hundred not-for-profit programs in the community, including school and church-outreach projects, family foundations and philanthropic establishments.

Residents support all types of causes from ALS (known as Lou Gehrig's disease) to WINGS (a program for women and children who have survived domestic violence), Relay for Life, hospice, Giving Day, the Barrington 220 School Foundation, the Barrington Area Community Foundation, the Lions Club, Kiwanis Club and Rotary International (breakfast and noon clubs).

*Above*: Barrington's Rotary International supports numerous local organizations.

*Right*: Churches throughout the community sponsor free meals throughout the year. The programs are well received and enjoyed by all who attend.

Thousands and thousands of dollars are collected every year by Barrington residents who walk, ride, dine, ski, serve or spend a day helping out at charity events. These volunteers have much in common: a drive to aid fellow citizens and a desire to make the world better, safer and more secure for now and for future generations.

One unique fundraising arm of the community is the Alpine Children's Charity. The program was begun by a group of teenagers to provide research for juvenile diabetes, Children's Heart (disease) Foundation and the Bear Necessities Pediatric Cancer Foundation. Over the past several years, these young people have raised over $1 million for the three charities with their yearly ski event held in Vail, Colorado. These young people are just the beginning of Barrington's charitable aims.

The list of Barrington' s guardian angels is long. Some of the most notable philanthropists include Norval Stephens, Bob Lee, Roxy and Richard Pepper, Freddie Pederson, Jan Karon (Giving Day), Vicky Wauterlek (Hands of Hope) and Kim Duchossois.

The Barrington Area Community Foundation or BACF was established in 1998 to grant seed money to charitable organizations for the purpose of initiating or expanding Barington and other community programs and projects whose needs are unmet in other ways. Norval Stephens's vision for the BACF organization took root in the fall of 1997 when he invited his friend Jim Lancaster to meet him at Egg Harbor for breakfast to discuss an idea Stephens had. After their meeting, Lancaster knew that Stephens was on to something unique, grand and glorious.

While attending an out-of-state conference, Stephens became inspired to start a group devoted to direct community service. After breakfast and support from Lancaster, Stephens set the wheels in motion to establish the Barrington Area Community Foundation. Next came the selection of others to serve on the board. He chose Kim Duchossois, Jim Fitzgerald, David Nelson, Glenn Reed and George Yapp for the job, each successful fundraisers in their own right.

Norval Stephens, the consummate volunteer and philanthropist, put Barrington on the map with his giving philosophy. *Portrait courtesy of Thomas Balsamo.*

The primary goal of BACF was to addresses a wide range of glaring community wants in the realms of human services, healthcare, education, art and culture, the environment and economic development. BACF was launched the following September. Its first grant awarded $5,000 in 2000. Since that time, the organization has committed to granting 5 percent of its assets on a five-year rolling average. To date, BACF has invested $994,390 in community projects.

Stephens was born on the south side of Chicago and earned degrees at DePauw and the University of Chicago, where he obtained a master's degree in business. Norval Stephens is emblematic of America's giving spirit. He has devoted much of his life to giving back to the schools he attended, the church where he worships, the community where he lives and the country he loves when he served it during the Korean Conflict. Many consider him the ultimate volunteer. Stephens's exemplary military career with the marine corps earned him the position of highly admired administrator of those under his command, and he held the rank of captain when he retired. He and his wife, Diane, moved to Barrington's Fox Point in the 1980s. In 2001, Stephens was chosen as an Outstanding Foundation Volunteer by the North American Interfraternity Conference for the numerous times he sat on boards and because of his work as a fundraiser and as a role model for leadership for a variety of organizations, from Rotary International to DePauw University and the Barrington Methodist Church. Friends and colleagues describe Stephens as genuine, caring, supportive, committed and an outstanding organizer. Those who know and work with Stephens revere him as "an officer and a gentleman." Many consider Norval Stephens a gift to Barrington.

Vicky Wauteriek created Hands of Hope after an eye-opening 1999 trip to Nigeria, where she was inspired to aid women and children by founding a 100 percent not-for-profit organization to fund humanitarian projects overseas. The annual spring Barrington Country Garden & Antique Faire became its signature fundraising event. All proceeds provide projects for Nigerian women and children that include building wells and schools, providing loans for agricultural projects and making resources available to enable women in Sub-Saharan Africa to become economically self-sustaining.

Another Barrington philanthropic benefactor is the Pepper family, a quiet and unassuming couple whose gifts reach many people in many directions. Richard Pepper's grandparents came to America to seek a better life for their children and to attain the American dream. Arthur Frederick Pepper and his wife, Nellye Luke Pepper, took separate paths to America and met in Chicago. At this time, many Brits were headed for Canada, where they

Roxy and Richard Pepper represent one of Barrington's most consistent benefactors. Already, they have left an impressive legacy in their adopted hometown. *Photo courtesy of the Pepper family.*

would be familiar with its culture and customs. How or by what means the Peppers arrived in America, in Chicago, is unknown. However, searching for employment seems to have been a primary motivation for the Peppers to come to the city. New buildings were popping up throughout the area, and job opportunities were plentiful for workers with healthy appetites to better their lots.

By the late 1920s, Chicago and the rest of the nation were headed for a depression. Fortunately for Richard's father, Stanley, Marshall Field wanted to move much of his merchandise to the Merchandise Mart, a new mammoth structure on the banks of the Chicago River. Field wondered if Stanley's Pepper Construction Company could do the job. Of course it could! On a personal level, even bigger news was that the Peppers had added a baby boy to their family, taking a place alongside his sister, Carol.

On June 23, 1930, Richard Pepper joined the family. Little did the infant know the plans his proud father had for him. Soon after his son's birth, Stanley moved his home office into a small space on Lawrence Avenue.

Stanley continued working at the Merchandise Mart building spaces as Field commissioned them.

Later, Field added the Pepper Construction Company to his team as builders of new stores and renovators of existing buildings and put them in charge of setting up Field's magical animated Christmas windows. The mutually beneficial partnership continued for decades.

In no time, Stan established a reputation as a no-nonsense businessman who would get the job done in the most professional terms. He taught his son, Richard, these skills. The young boy would continue adding to his father's admirable work reputation.

By 1937, Stan was taking on jobs outside Chicago, first building twenty single-family homes in Glenview. It was about this time that the Peppers purchased a getaway retreat at Pistakee Bay near the Wisconsin border. As soon as school was dismissed for the summer, Grace took her children north. There they spent their vacations swimming, sailing and socializing. Stan joined his family whenever he could break away from the office.

In 1939, the Peppers moved to a home in Arlington Heights and later moved to a farmhouse in Inverness, where they lived for eighteen years. Richard's parents, Stan and Grace, sent him to school in Barrington for grades six to eight. After his middle school years in Barrington, Richard elected to attend Palatine High School, where he excelled in football and basketball. His father had hoped that Richard would go to a private high school, but he declined. When Richard graduated in 1948, there was no doubt where Richard was headed for college. It would be Northwestern in Evanston. Richard elected to study engineering—that way he would have the best of both worlds: his father's drive and business acumen and a college degree that would provide him with the tools to compete with other construction companies.

Northwestern proved to be a game changer for Richard, for it was there that he met his future bride, Roxy. Born in Chicago on June 14, 1932, Roxy was the oldest of three children born to James R. and Harriet B. Miller. When Roxy was nine, her family moved from Chicago to Wilmette, a short distance from the university. Her father became dean of the Medical School but took a leave to serve his country during World War II at the Bureau of Medicine and Surgery at Bethesda, Maryland. Returning to Northwestern after his war duties, Miller was elected president of Northwestern, a role he held for twenty-five years.

Carol, Richard's sister, introduced him to Roxy. Their first date in Chicago was to hear a Dixieland band. The young couples often double-dated.

Richard remembers, "I don't think people realized that she [Roxy] was the president's daughter; Roxy was just one of the group." Everyone was smitten by Roxy's warmth, charm and thoughtfulness. The couple became engaged over Christmas during their junior year and were married on September 6, 1952, before they began their senior year at Northwestern. Richard graduated with a degree in civil engineering and Roxy with a degree in speech correction.

At twenty-two, Richard joined his father's booming construction business. With the Korean conflict still raging, Richard took the naval officer's training exam. After the exam, he was scheduled to report in July to the naval center at Newport, Rhode Island. Since they were expecting their first child in August, Richard asked for a deferment. It was granted. On August 29, 1952, James Stanley Pepper was born. Soon afterward, the Korean conflict came to a halt.

Richard returned to his job with the Pepper Construction Company, but his always-proper father felt his son still had more lessons to learn, and when Richard reported to work sporting a navy-blue blazer, gray flannel trousers, loafers and a dress shirt and tie, Stanley told his son that Pepper management wore dark suits, not preppy fashions. Many more and different lessons were still to be learned.

Over the next several decades, Richard's learning curve with his father's company allowed him to take on more jobs and more responsibilities. Meanwhile, alongside Richard, more children were added to the family. In 1960, the Peppers bought land and built their home in Barrington. With rolling hills and two lakes, the property was the perfect place for the Peppers' growing family. In her book *Pepper Construction: Beyond Bricks and Mortar* Ann B. Gowman wrote, "The Pepper children became good friends with each other and have some four-legged pals as well."

The book recounts Missy, a golden retriever that was one of their most memorable pets. "She started off her day…by running down the long stretch of driveway to fetch the paper…and later, when the children were ready for school, Missy made another trek down the driveway to watch them board the bus. She was also waiting for them when they returned home." Barrington was a good mix for the Peppers; the family continued to grow (eventually to six children: Stan, David, Scot, Lisa, Richard and Lynda), and so did Pepper Construction Company (with work for All State Insurance, numerous churches, shopping malls, two structures at Epcot, a stint in Saudi Arabia and work in Texas). Pepper Construction has left its "footprint" far and wide. While the company prospered, the Peppers have always given.

In 2001, Northwestern University awarded Richard and Roxy the school's highest alumni honor for their ongoing donations to the school campus and programs. Other institutions and causes have earned the Peppers' benevolence, including Habitat for Humanity, conservation projects, hospitals, museums, gardens, orchestras, art centers, scouting programs, local schools and schools of higher learning, as well as a hospice care facility.

The senior Peppers have blessed Barrington in countless ways: among their most visible works are the award-winning Garland complex, Journey Care (formerly Hospice of Northeastern Illinois) and the Barrington Park District's Forever Young Tree House, a place for people of all ages and abilities to celebrate the outdoors and enjoy special gatherings.

To quote Northwestern publication *Of Good Report, Winter, 1993*, "While some people scan the horizon and see a thin, flat line, others imagine contours vastly different. Such is the legacy of Roxy and Richard Pepper; to be among the visionaries and planners, the shapers and builders of a bold, new world."

Most of us have read a book that changed our lives. Who doesn't remember reading *Gone With the Wind*, *A Tale of Two Cities* or one of the *Harry Potter* books? While reading Mitch Albom's book *Tuesdays with Morrie*, Barrington's Bob Lee had an epiphany. Near retirement, he asked himself what he wanted to do with the rest of his life. The answer was simple: he wanted to make a difference and hoped to combine his desire to be of service to others with his joy of riding his bike. With gratitude for his own good health, Lee desired to help others and serve as a spokesperson for ALS patients who, as the disease advances, become speechless. Thus, Bob began his charity, Ride for 3 Reasons.

Along his journeys, Bob met and got to know several people living with ALS. In a *Daily Herald* interview with Bill O'Brien, Lee said, "To me, it's the most dreadful thing you can be diagnosed with." He added, "Imagine what it must feel like to lose control of your muscles, your ability to move and speak and eventually to breathe." Like a kite on a journey, Lee cycled the perimeter of our country on three different rides. In 2001, he rode 3,200 miles in sixty-three days along the southern U.S. border and raised $86,000. His 2007 ride needed 650 donors to garner a $65,000 grant from the Duchossois Family Foundation. He got the grant. Lee's second ride took him to the East, where he rode from Flordia to Maine and then flew to Seattle and rode back to Maine. This ride totaled 6,500 miles to celebrate his sixty-fifth birthday. Ride number three came in 2012 after Lee participated in an ice cream sundae send-off from the Wool Street Grill and Sports Bar.

Bob Lee says that he had three reasons to ride across America. They are to raise funds for ALS, cancer and hospice. As the volunteer's ode reminds us, "What you have done for others is yours forever." *Photo courtesy of Bob Lee.*

This trip started on September 5 as Lee headed off on a 2,000-mile trek from Vancouver, Canada, to the Mexico border. Each expedition had two goals: raising funds and raising awareness. "Dollars may lead to cures, but stories breed awareness," commented Lee.

In pursuit of making others aware, Lee cycled twelve thousand miles. "Through my involvement with the RIDES and charities, I have met countless people who inspired me to move forward every day," says Lee. "The RIDE is a journey that allowed me to touch people's lives in a meaningful way while also engaging my lifelong dream of traveling America's back roads."

Lee's odysseys have attracted ride followers, donors, researchers and volunteers from forty-two states and seven countries. His journeys have moved well beyond the back roads. He has appeared on numerous talk shows, in countless print media and at civic events across the country. Lee paid his own expenses and donated 100 percent of the $1.3 million raised to the three charities: ALS, hospice and cancer. Bob Lee is a force to be reckoned with, an inspiration for all.

In May 2007, the Barrington Giving Day was inaugurated as a not-for-profit. Each year since, families and individuals who qualify for the free and reduced lunch program are invited to attend Barrington's Giving Day at Station Middle School on Eastern Avenue. Here they can select needed items for the upcoming winter and holiday season. Many months go into preparing for the Giving Day. Community groups, students, businesses and churches gather food, coats, hats, gloves, toys, gifts and much more to hand out to needy families and individuals. Approximately 350 families are served. There is a large contingent of students who work the day alongside over three hundred adult volunteers. Setup begins Friday night with help from the Barrington High School Pom Pons, the Lions Club, the Youth Board, the BHS football team, the National Junior Honor Society and others. By Saturday, the parking lot, side streets and circle drive around the middle school are packed with cars. Families arrive early to select what they need. Shopping carts are available, and the goods are carried out to and loaded into their cars.

The Barrington Education Foundation provides district schools with projects and programs not covered by the school district's budget. Founded in 1999, the Barrington 220 Educational Foundation has raised over $2 million for the school district. Carol McGregor has been on the foundation's board since its inception. She said in a 2014 article in *Quintessential Magazine*, "We [board members] were all from the community to begin with and we all had a connection to the schools." The foundation was guided by Glen Gerard, a Michigan-based education and business agency that led the group to determine its leadership organization, its bylaws and its function.

The first project undertaken by the foundation was the T.R. Youngstrom Memorial High Ropes and Climbing Wall at Barrington High School. T.R. was a graduate of BHS who was so inspired by his BHS photography class that he moved to Colorado to go to college and to take photos of the area's sport's venues. In no time, the gifted photographer's work appeared in countless magazines—*Climbing Magazine* (his first shots), *Powder, GQ, Skiing, ELLE, Bike* and *Snowboard Life* to name a few. T.R. died while on assignment in Chile in 1997, but his spirit is alive and well in Barrington.

The foundation's first chairperson was Dede Wamberg, a former District 220 board member. The group's plan was to make personal contacts with potential donors—no cold calls. It worked—in no time, the foundation was viable. The foundation divides its funds into four categories: PIE Grants (Projects for Innovation and Enhancement), Helping Hands Grants designed to provide teachers with up to $500 for classroom needs not covered by the schools' budgets, community speakers and major projects that have included a Four Seasons mural painted by local artist Susan Hanson and is in the foyer of the Early Learning Center. The realistic painting enables two- to five-year-olds to learn about the changing seasons even before they are able to read about them. Other projects funded for the schools include books, art kits, math games, a school vegetable garden, fitness equipment and more. The foundation works closely with the administration and teachers to address their classroom needs.

The project-funded wish list takes about nine months to be delivered. It is a very democratic process with input from many directions. Funds are collected in a variety of ways, from direct mailing solicitations to golf outings and special participatory dinners at one of the local country clubs. Regarding the purpose of the foundation, Katherine Logue likes to remind donors that taxpayers' dollars go only so far. She also reminds them that Barrington has excellent schools and being "one of the best" costs money.

A consummate Barrington philanthropist is Frederica (Freddie) Herriman Smith Pederson. She recalls growing up in Barrington as tranquil and full of fun. Freddie and her brother and sister were "always active and

T.R. Youngstrom, Distinguished Graduate of BHS, was a well-published photographer focusing on outdoor sports and Colorado's natural beauty. He died while on assignment in Chile in a helicopter crash in 1997.

outside." Her parents, Claude Danforth Herriman and Helene Hoffman Herriman, taught their children to be "strong and courteous." Pederson followed her parents' teachings. She gives generously to causes in her town and funds programs that she deems effective, such as Journey Care and Barrington Area Council on Aging (BACOA), where Freddie served on the board. She served on the board of the Barrington Community Foundation for six years and is now a life member of the board. Freddie also donated the bridge built in her late husband, Keith Pederson's, name that connects Citizens Park to Cuba Marsh. In addition, she gave land in his name to the Conservation Trust for the Pederson Preserve, as Keith was an avid outdoor enthusiast and conservationist at heart. Freddie wrote a substantial personal check to the American Cancer Society when a neighbor walking the subdivision and collecting for the organization knocked on her door and asked for a donation. Freddie is a lovely, soft-spoken woman whose warmth radiates to all with whom she comes in contact.

Don Thompson Sr. moved to Barrington from Palatine in 1940. In 1943, he enlisted in the army and served in its Twenty-seventh Division stationed in the Pacific. Thompson was awarded a Bronze Star and a Purple Heart when he was wounded in Okinawa. He returned home on December 7, 1945. Soon after that, Thompson joined the American Legion and became a charter member of VFW Post 7706. He served as commander of the organization and was actively involved in its many charitable events. When the post began taking a direct role in supporting patients at the Veterans Affairs Medical Center in North Chicago, Thompson made it his duty to inform local and unaware vets of their right to receive annual physicals and medical supplies from North Chicago. Once a week, he would drive people to the center, especially helping those who weren't able to drive themselves. The sprawling North Chicago complex can be daunting for those going there for the first time. Thompson's mission was to ease them into and around the labyrinth maze of buildings. He checked them into the reception area and saw that they received proper documentation and assisted them in completing all the necessary paperwork in order to receive services. In addition to being a chauffer, Thompson and other post members used money they earned from their sloppy joe dinners and golf outings to purchase equipment used by the staff and patients on a regular basis. On one trip to the hospital, Thompson noticed patients lying in bed with no TVs, no fans and no access to ice machines. He thought, "Gee, that could be me." So he and fellow post members Burnell Wollar and Larry Popp decided that they would go every Tuesday to visit with those confined to bed.

*Left*: Freddie donated land to honor her late husband, Keith. The Pederson Preserve is situated at the intersection of Hart and Lake Cook Roads.

*Below*: Diminutive and soft-spoken Freddie Pederson has blessed Barrington with numerous acts of support from Journey Care to the Council on Aging and helping a neighbor collecting funds for the American Cancer Society. *Photo courtesy of Thomas Balsamo.*

According to Kenneth List, chief of community affairs, "This group is a very easy group to work with. The fact that [patients] know someone cares to visit them has to be a plus." Thompson donated 4,148 hours and twenty years of attention to the VA program that provided patients with blankets, clothing and TVs. Don Thompson Sr. knew on a personal level the importance of

*Top*: Eugene (Gene) Dawson stands outside the Barrington Township office with two colleagues. The township provides nonperishable goods to those in need.

*Above, left*: Don Thompson Sr., still sporting his World War II army uniform, stands next to his son, Don Thompson Jr., renowned principal of Barrington Middle School Station Campus and, later, BMS Prairie Campus.

*Above, right*: Bill Hannay, dressed in Civil War garb, represents all Barrington residents who have answered the nation's call to duty. Hannay appeared at the Sesquicentennial Memorial Day Parade at Evergreen Cemetery.

giving back to others, especially to his fellow "band of brothers." During his life, Thompson received many honors for his service to Barrington and to his country, including induction into the Senior Citizens Hall of Fame (2003), Lincoln Day Ceremonies (2009), Department of Veterans Affairs—Community Affairs Certificates (1999, 2000 and 2002) and a VFW Certificate of Commendation for twenty years of "service, loyalty and generosity to the post" from the State of Illinois, House of Representatives "in recognition of Your dedication to the Barrington Community and your service to the Barrington Memorial Post VFW 7706" and a "Heritage of Freedom Award in Appreciation for your Participation in the Village of Barrington 1995 4th of July Parade." To quote Attorney David Alms in a letter to Fran Thompson, Don's bride, "Both Don and yourself have been very influential in the type of person I have become and set standards for me I still attempt to achieve. Your belief and confidence in me while I was in high school and college and now as a practicing attorney has given me the base I needed to succeed." Don Thompson Sr. served as a generous role model to many in our community.

In addition to the kindness of many Barrington individuals, the township provides nonperishable goods to those in need throughout the year.

# Bibliography

Allen, Nancy P. *The Barrington Area Library*. Barrington, IL, 1976.

"Author [Veronica Roth] Makes Hometown Appearance." *Suburban Life*. October 10, 2013.

Baizerman, Suzanne, ed. *Marvin Lipofsky: A Glass Odyssey*. Oakland: Oakland Museum of California, 2003.

Balgemann, Bob. "Voice of State Wrestling." Undated newspaper clipping.

Balsamo, Thomas. I Have a Voice. Traveling gallery show launched 2009.

Balsamo, Thomas, and Sharon Rosenbloom. *Souls: Beneath and Beyond Autism*. New York: McGraw Hill, 2004.

*Barrington Courier Review*. "Deborah Cooke—Spear Points." October 17, 1970.

*Barrington High School Alumni Directory, 2009*. Barrington, IL: Harris Connect, 2009.

Barrington Historical Society. *A Date With History*. Barrington, IL: Holke Press, 1988, 1990 and 1991.

Barrington Press Publication. "History Is Made in the Union of Two Denominations." May 16, 1968.

*Barrington Regional Magazine*. Barrington Area Chamber of Commerce, 2010, 2012, 2013.

*Barrington Township Reporter*. May 2009.

Barrington United School District 220. *Profiles in Excellence from District 220*. Annual Review. 2003.

Bartlett, John. *Familiar Quotations*. 16th ed. Boston: Little, Brown and Company, 1992.

Benson Barbara L. *They Builded Better Than They Knew: Historical Perspective of the Barrington Area*. N.p.: Barrington Area Development Council, 2003.

Bielski, Ursula. *More Chicago Haunts, Scenes from Myths and Memories*. Chicago: Lake Claremont Press, 2000.

*Daily Herald*. JFK photos. November 22, 2015.

Ditka, Mike. *The '85 Bears (25th Anniversary—We Were the Greatest)*. Chicago: Triumph Books, 2005.

Editors of Life. *The First World War: A Portfolio of Famous Paintings & Posters*. New York: Time, Inc., 1964.

Fard, Barbara E. "His Work Takes on a Peaceful Hue." *Daily Herald*, November 17, 1985.

Frisk, Bob. "Tom Frederick's Battle Brings Career into Focus." *Daily Herald*, n.d.

"Gary Fencik, the Bear from Barrington." *Illinois Entertainer*, January 1986.

Heitman, Karl. Barrington's First Train Station, Parts 1 and 2. March 8, 2015, and February 14, 2015. https://www.youtube.com/watch?v=8AHwGwUQYgM and https://www.youtube.com/watch?v=-4Jw1CMITww&feature=youtu.be.

———. Barrington's Octagon House. March 8, 2015. https://www.youtube.com/watch?v=T0Oqfo2QfCM&feature=youtu.be.

———. The Catlow Puppet Theater. March 8, 2015. https://www.youtube.com/watch?v=nzaJayeA4Vw&feature=youtu.be.

Hillenbrand, Laura. *Unbroken*. New York: Random House, 2010.

Hilton, Robert. *The Story of Jewel's Move to Barrington*. Chicago: Jewel Tea Co., Inc., 1929.

*History of Barrington*. Arnett C. Lines Collection, Barrington Area Library.

Hybels, Bill. *Just Walk Across the Room*. Grand Rapids, MI: Zondervan, 2006.

Johnson, Tom. "CFC Gains More Land to Preserve." *Barrington Courier Review*. December 15, 2005.

———. "Willow Creek Focused on Future as It Marks 30 Years." *Barrington Courier Review*. December 1, 2005.

Keegan, John. *The First World War*. New York: Alfred A. Knopf, 1999.

Knisley, Michael. *Pro Football's Greatest Teams*. St. Louis, MO.: Sporting News, 2002.

Mee, Charles. *A Nearly Normal Life*. New York: Little, Brown and Company, 1999.

Peterson, Eric. "VFW: Vets Take a Personal Interest." *Daily Herald*, April 21, 2001.

*Quarterly Northwest Business Magazine*. Spring 2010 and Fall 2012.

*Quintessential Barrington*. 2005–2014. Available at the Barrington Area Library.

Sharp, Cynthia. *Tales of Old Barrington*. Barrington Area Bicentennial Commission and the Barrington Press, Inc., 1976.

"Star Soprano." *Pioneer Press*, October 2001.

Stevens, C.M. *The True Story of the Great European War*. Chicago: Hamming Pub. Co., 1914.

Throne, Tarah. "Father-Son Team Helps Charities." *Barrington Suburban Life*, December 1913.

VanHagen, George. *A Salute to the Military History of Barrington*. Barrington, IL, 2008.

Walaitis, Edward. *Chicago Tribune*. March 2, 2005, 12.

Wearin, Itha D. *Along Country Roads*. N.p.: Wallace-Homestead Book Company, 1976.

Westhoff, Jeffrey. "Allison, Arthur and an Olympic Dream." *Quintessential Barrington*, July/August 2012.

Whitehouse, David. *Glass: A Short History*. Washington, D.C.: Smithsonian Books, 2012.

# Index

# About the Author

*Portrait by Thomas Balsamo.*

Diane P. Kostick has lived in Barrington for more than fifty years. She and her husband, Andy, raised two children, Yuri and Jolie, in the village. She taught language arts in Barrington Unit School District 220 for thirty-nine years and now teaches courses in both U.S. history and humanities at the Illinois Institute of Art in Schaumburg. She has won numerous awards, including Who's Who Among American Teachers (twice); was nominated for WTTW's Golden Apple Award (twice); was Teacher of the Year in Illinois for the International Academy of Design and Technology IADT (third in the nation); was the Barrington Area Library representative for its Illinois Authors Celebration; was named Barrington Township Senior Citizen; and received the Kohl's Foundation International Award for Exemplary Teaching.

She has traveled extensively in the United States, Canada and Europe. The family has always hosted interesting guests and continues to entertain their friends from all over the world. In 1977, Kostick launched a Back-to-Back French Exchange Program, which was supported by the community for twenty-five years.

Kostick has been a member of the Barrington Writer's Workshop and the Second Saturday Poetry Workshop for decades and is the author of eight books. A more recent work, *Voices of Barrington*, was subtitled "From the Barber to the Billionaire" and profiled nine outstanding people who came from remarkable and varied backgrounds—young and mature, men and women—whose influences helped shape the Barrington community.

Her *Chronicles of Barrington, Illinois* focuses on many more of these extraordinary citizens who contributed to Barrington's rich history. *Chronicles* archives a fascinating story, leading the reader from the early prairie settlement in the tiny village to its current life encompassing Barrington, Barrington Hills, Deer Park, Inverness, Lake Barrington, North Barrington, Port Barrington, South Barrington and Tower Lakes.

# About the Artists

Mort Luby's art-competition awards number in excess of fifty, including Best-of-Show citations. His paintings are displayed worldwide in both corporate and private collections.

Luby works in watercolor and oil, often in the plein-air tradition, painting his landscapes on location. His composition won first place in the 2014 Quick-Paint Division at the Woodstock Plein Air competition. He won both the People's Choice and the Artist's Choice first-place awards at the 2013 "Art in Nature" event in Barrington.

He received his education at the Universities of Wisonsin and Notre Dame, earning a bachlor of arts degree. In addition, Luby has studied at the Art Institute of Chicago, the Palette and Chisel Academy of Art and the Scottsdale Artists' School. He has attended workshops with America's premier artists, including Romel de la Torre, Charles Movali, Alvaro Castagnet, Margaret Kessler, Dian Johnson, Tony Couch and many others.

He is a member of the Plein Air Painters of Hawaii, the Plein Air Painters of Chicago, the Palette and Chisel Academy and several other art groups.

Mort lives in Carpentersville, Illinois, but spends every winter on the island of Maui, where four galleries showcase his paintings. He is represented at four additional galleries and stores in the Chicago area.

Thomas Balsamo is a nationally recognized artistic portrait photographer. On Saturday, May 6, 2015, at the Sanfilippo Estate, Balsamo was presented with its Humanitarian Award for his use of his art to educate and benefit others. More than two hundred guests attended the event to honor Balsamo's lifetime achievements. He is profiled in Chapter 3.